Elizabethan and Jacobean Pamphlets

by Various

ISBN: 9781318081042

Copyright © 2016 by HardPress

HardPress
8345 NW 66TH ST #2561
MIAMI FL 33166-2626
USA
Email: info@hardpress.net

Ordering Information:

Quantity sales. Special discounts are available on quantity purchases by corporations, associations, and others. For details, contact the publisher by email at the address above.

Printed in the United States of America, United Kingdom and Australia

Demy 16mo, 3s. 6d. each. Bound in paper boards, with parchment back.

THE POCKET LIBRARY

OF

ENGLISH LITERATURE

Edited by GEORGE SAINTSBURY

A collection, in separate volumes, partly of extracts from long books, partly of short pieces, by the same writer, on the same subject, or of the same class.

Vol. I.—Tales of Mystery.
II.—Political Verse.
III.—Defoe's Minor Novels.
IV.—Political Pamphlets.
V.—Seventeenth Century Lyrics.
VI.—Elizabethan And Jacobean Pamphlets.

LONDON: PERCIVAL & CO.

ELIZABETHAN & JACOBEAN PAMPHLETS EDITED BY

GEORGE SAINTSBURY

LONDON
PERCIVAL AND CO.
1892

CONTENTS

		PAGE
	INTRODUCTION	vii
I.	THOMAS LODGE.	
	Reply to Gosson	1
II.	JOHN LYLY (?)	
	Pap with a Hatchet	43
III.	NICHOLAS BRETON.	
	A Pretty and Witty Discourse	84
IV.	ROBERT GREENE.	
	Groat's Worth of Wit	115

V.	GABRIEL HARVEY.	
	Precursor to Pierce's Supererogation	164
VI.	THOMAS NASH.	
	Prognostication	185
VII.	THOMAS DEKKER.	
	The Gull's Hornbook	209
	NOTES	277

INTRODUCTION

I can conceive some readers, not necessarily frivolous, anticipating little pleasure from a volume devoted to examples of Elizabethan and Jacobean pamphlets. It must be the business of the volume I have planned to convince them that they are wrong. But even before that volume is read, I think it not impossible to show cause for its right to exist. The originals of these pamphlets, except a few which have become familiar in consequence of their bearing on Shakespearian questions, were till recently almost unknown, except to a few scholars and antiquaries, and are still for the most part inaccessible except in the original editions, which are bought at large prices by collectors, or in limited and often privately issued modern reprints. Yet their interest is very great. The pamphlet of the late sixteenth and early seventeenth[Pg viii] century corresponded much more nearly to the modern periodical than to anything else, unless, indeed, it be the modern newspaper. It included fiction, sketches of society, accounts of travel, literary criticism, personal controversy, theology,—the whole farrago, in short, of the non-political columns of our journals. It was in many cases written by men of much greater talent than the average journalist of the present day. In one remarkable case—that of the so-called Martin Marprelate controversy—it holds a position almost unique, or only shared by the not wholly dissimilar groups of literature which included and grew up round Pascal's *Provinciales* and the *Tracts for the Times*. Above all, it has the advantage of a singular variety of subject, and of presenting the opportunity of making a great number of lively extracts, certainly faithful to the manners of the time, and showing those manners in a fashion not easy to surpass in freshness, contrast of colour, and incisive outline.

The pamphlet was one of the most immediate and necessary creations of the printing press. Before that invention it was hardly possible, and a very considerable time had to elapse afterwards before the combination of education in the reader, command of mechanical means in the diffuser, and changed[Pg ix] political conditions, enabled the newspaper to supplant it. The pamphlet, so far as production is concerned, when once private presses are accessible, gives few hostages to fortune or to the strong hand of authority. It may make but a single appearance, and then the type is broken up, the machinery removed, and the printed copies left to find their way and do their work. A newspaper must have more or less of a headquarters, definite managers, at the very least a regular place and time of appearance at which it can be waited for and snapped up. Of the advantages offered by the pamphlet there is a good example in the fact that under the active, intelligent, and almost despotic government of Elizabeth, though the Martin Marprelate tracts excited the intensest hatred not merely of the lay authorities but of a powerful and omnipresent ecclesiastical corporation, the presses were only once (at Newton Lane in Lancashire) discovered and seized. In less perilous matter the pamphlet, if it did not give so much protection, 'obliged' even less. Its cost was small; the author was in no way bound to follow it up with anything else. It took him but a little time to produce; its profit, if there was any, came in quickly; it could be sold out before pirates could get hold of it; it did not frighten the unlearned by bulk and[Pg x] pretensions. On the other hand, of course, it had its drawbacks. It was of its nature, and in more points than one of that nature, ephemeral. The chances were rather against than in favour of its being preserved; for even in these days when most people have a library or book-room of some kind, the very student himself acknowledges with gnashings of teeth the way things published in pamphlet form have of 'going under,' of simply disappearing, he cannot tell how or whither. Hence the real and intrinsic interest of the pamphlet has had added to it the accidental and factitious interest of rarity. It is hardly a paradox to say that one of the best chances which such a thing had of surviving was the fact of its being proscribed and burnt by the hangman. There was then some reason for treasuring it instead of letting it go to clean boots, light fires, and wrap pounds of butter.

The pamphlets of the Elizabethan age were almost as often in verse as in prose, the superior attraction of verse for early and uncultivated audiences not having died out. Indeed, far later than the period covered by this volume, things continued to be written in verse which were merely pamphlets, and gave us both matter of eternity, such as *Absalom and Achitophel*[Pg xi] or *Religio Laici*, and hard-bound doggerel like Defoe's *True-Born Englishman* and *Jure Divino*. The Elizabethan verse pamphlet, which was largely written by Thomas Churchyard, Nicholas Breton, John Davies, Samuel Rowlands, and others, is a curiosity, but as a rule very little more; and I do not propose to give any examples of it here. Nor, the space at my command being all too limited, have I thought it necessary to draw in this present volume on the miscellaneous pamphlets of the times. The examples will be taken from what may be called the great single pamphleteers or pamphlet collections—that is to say, Lodge, Greene, Nash, Harvey, 'Martin Marprelate' and the anti-Martinists, Breton, and Dekker. Some particulars of each of the selected authors or groups may appropriately be given in this introduction.

No minor Elizabethan author is better known than Robert Greene, partly from the fact that he touches Shakespeare, and partly from the other fact that his short and ill-spent life was that of the typical Bohemian, and so interests those who like gossip about men of letters. He was born in 1560 at Norwich, was educated at Clare Hall, Cambridge (being also subsequently incorporated at Oxford), travelled on the Continent, married, treated his wife very badly, may[Pg xii] have been both a clerk in orders and a student of medicine, lived recklessly in London as a dramatist and pamphleteer, and died at the age of thirty-two either *propter* or merely *post* undue consumption of pickled herrings and Rhenish wine. His plays, though full of the ante-Shakespearian crudity and unskilled workmanship, have many graceful touches; the songs which he scattered about both his plays and his poems are frequently charming; his pamphlets, which, short as his life was, are very numerous, perhaps rank, on the whole, above those of any other Elizabethan writer for combined bulk, variety, and merit. They were produced in the space of about ten years (1583-92). Those certainly known to be his, or probably attributed to him, are nearly thirty in number, and almost defy classification. Some of them approach that strange type of novel consisting of a minimum of story, a maximum of moralising, and, if I may say so, a *plusquam*-maximum of conceited style, the example of which had been set in Lyly's *Euphues*. Not a few are personal reminiscences—how far deliberately imbued with an exaggerated profession of repentance in order to hit readers with both barrels it is very hard to say. A distinct and very interesting set deals with the ways of the Eliza[Pg xiii]bethan 'conny-catcher,' the 'Captain Rook' (though usually of lower grade) of the time. Others are pure book-making, as we should call it now, about subjects which for political or other reasons happened to be in the public eye at the moment. Greene is certainly one of the most typical of his fellowship.

With him and close to him may be ranked Thomas Lodge, who was his contemporary, and for a time his comrade; but who, unlike Greene, settled down as a Roman Catholic physician, and outliving the hapless 'Roberto' more than thirty years, did not die till the last year of James. Lodge had perhaps higher powers than Greene, except in drama. One of his pamphlets, 'Rosalynde' or 'Euphues' Golden Legacy', gave Shakespeare, as most people now know, the subject of *As You Like It*, and has been more than once reprinted for that reason. He had also a faculty of which Greene shows no trace whatever—that of an accomplished literary critic; and twice, in answer to Gosson and Campion, took the right side against some of the literary heresies which animated that active and fruitful time. He was decidedly best in the euphuist romance, but he also practised the social satire pamphlet with no small success.

[Pg xiv]

Nash and Harvey shared with Greene the luck, good or other, of being earlier presented in their lives, and in at least some of their works, to modern writers than their fellows. Indeed, Greene's not wholly enviable fame is as much due to the quarrels of these two as to his own works. Gabriel Harvey, the elder but very much the less able of the two, was a Fellow of Pembroke College, Cambridge, a friend of Sidney and of Spenser (whose *Faërie Queene* he unmercifully snubbed, preferring the curious fancy of classical metres which was long patronised by the 'Areopagus' or Sidneian clique), and a man of real scholarship. But his exemplification of the worst faults of the university prig, and the pitiless exposure of them in his controversy with Thomas Nash (a younger Cambridge man, and wielder of the sharpest and most unscrupulous pen of his time), have brought down such hard language on him from most literary historians that one or two charitable or paradoxical souls have been tempted to take up the cudgels on his side. To this length, I cannot go. Why Harvey and Nash quarrelled no one knows exactly; but the quarrel, the pamphlet results of which make up the greater part of Harvey's work, plays only a small part in that of Nash. The very quarrel itself had, or seems to have had, some[Pg xv]thing to do with the strange Marprelate business to be noticed presently, and Nash is at least with great probability supposed author of some of the chief numbers of that controversy on the anti-Martinist side. But he wrote not a little other pamphlet-matter, never quite attempting the euphuist romance in which his friends Greene and Lodge delighted, but producing discourses of apparitions in anticipation of Defoe, pious tractates expressing, or professing to express, his repentance for evil living, puffs (though this is rather an unkind word), such as his *Lenten Stuff*, eulogistic of the herrings which were the staple commodity of his native coast, and a curious book called *The Unfortunate Traveller*, dealing with the grand tour, and containing among other things the well-known romance (for romance it would seem to be) of Surrey the poet and his Geraldine. Where Nash stands eminent among the writers of the time is in his faculty of boisterous and burlesque abuse, which, in his famous lampoon upon Harvey, *Have with you to Saffron Walden* (Harvey's birthplace), displayed itself in a manner not easy to parallel elsewhere in English.

It is very hard to give in very brief space an account of the Martin Marprelate matter, yet without [Pg xvi] some such account extracts from it must be hardly intelligible. It began about the year 1588, chiefly owing to the action of a certain Reverend Nicholas Udall, a puritan divine who struck into the controversy between the Episcopal and Presbyterian parties in the Church, and embittered it by the use of language so violent that he himself was imprisoned and his printer's press seized. This printer, Waldegrave, enraged thereat, lent his art to members of the puritan sect even more violent than Udall (their exact identity is matter of controversy), and a fire of pamphlets was opened by them, the earliest being called *The Epistle* and *The Epitome*. In the first place, Dean Bridges of Salisbury and Bishop Cooper of Winchester, then other dignitaries, were assailed with real vigour and ability, but with the most unscrupulous partisanship, and in a dialect which for extravagance of abusive language had not been surpassed in the heat of the earlier Reformation controversies, and has scarcely been approached since. The partisans of the Church were fully equal to the occasion; and a counter fire of pamphlets, some of which are attributed with great probability to Nash, and others with hardly less to the Oxford dramatist and euphuist Lyly, was returned. The heat of the controversy lasted [Pg xvii] chiefly through three years—1588, 1589, and 1590; but it may be said in the widest sense to have endured for nearly seven—from 1586 to 1593, when Penry and Barrow, the supposed chiefs of the Martinists, were executed. Of the style of this singular controversy the extract will, I trust, give a sufficient idea. As to its matter, it is difficult to be more precise than this: that the object of the Martinist pamphleteers was to decry episcopacy by every possible description of personal abuse, applied to the holders and the defenders of the episcopal office, and that the object of their opponents of the same class (for men like Cooper and Bridges, still more like Whitgift and Hooker, stand in an entirely different category) was not so much to defend that office as to fling back in double measure the abuse upon 'Martin,' as the generic name went, and upon his known or supposed embodiments and partisans.

There can be few greater contrasts than between this furious ribaldry, as it too often is, and the mild mediocrity of Nicholas Breton. His claim to a place here (even if his merit be rated much lower than some have rated it) is, that he is the chief writer of the kind who is both in verse and prose a pamphleteer pure and simple. You cannot (at least I[Pg xviii] cannot) call Breton a poet, but he wrote immense quantities of verse, and in prose he pamphleted with such copiousness and persistence for nearly half a century, that it is clear there must have been money to be made by the practice.

The last of our chief single authors is Thomas Dekker, a very much greater man than Breton, though not so great in prose as in verse. He was somewhat later even in his beginning than the other writers I have noticed; and though his prose has not the formal merit or charm of his exquisite songs and his wonderful romantic character in drama, it is very interesting in matter. He paraphrases (*The Bachelor's Banquet*, *The Gull's Hornbook*) with remarkable freedom and skill; he chronicles plague years; he takes a hint from Greene, and extends and varies that author's satirical exposition of London tricks in a long and extremely vivid series of pamphlets, such as *The Bellman of London*, *The Seven Deadly Sins of London*, *Lanthorn and Candle Light*, *News from Hell*, and half a dozen others. In these, though of course a certain allowance must be made for the pressman's exaggeration in dealing with such subjects, there is a most singular and interesting picture of the lower and looser classes in England, at least in the English capital, at the time.

[Pg xix]

In this little book, after one or two changes of plan, I have finally decided on giving only entire pamphlets—a specimen of literary criticism from Lodge, of autobiographic romance from Greene, of politico-religious controversy from the Martin Marprelate series, of mingled self-panegyric and lampoon from Harvey, of burlesque from Nash, of paraphrase of foreign matter adapted to English conditions from Dekker, and of what may be called hack-work for the press from Breton. The annotation is deliberately limited to the removal of some of the most obvious stumbling-blocks to current reading. A full commentary on *The Gull's Hornbook* alone would fill another volume, and the object in these books is to give text not comment.

[Pg xx]
[Pg 1]

I.—THOMAS LODGE

(*Stephen Gosson's* Schoole of Abuse *has acquired something like fame in virtue of one of the answers to it—Sidney's* Defence of Poetry. *That interesting little book has been frequently reprinted of late, and some knowledge of it, and of Gosson's attack which caused it, may be taken as common. Lodge's attempt, made as a very young man, to do what Sidney did is far less familiar even to students. It was reprinted in 1853, and again in the rare and costly private issue by the Hunterian Club of Lodge's whole works; but the author of the introductory essay to that issue, my friend Mr. Gosse, has been somewhat unkind (I cannot say unjust) to it. It is, indeed, no great thing; but as a very early example of literary criticism by pamphlet, which has lacked the modern reprinting accorded to Webbe, Puttenham, Daniel, and other critics of the same time, I thought it might find appropriate place here.*)

[Pg 2]

A REPLY TO STEPHEN GOSSON'S SCHOOLE OF ABUSE IN DEFENCE OF POETRY, MUSICK, AND STAGE PLAYS.

Protogenes can know *Apelles* by his line though he se[e] him not, and wise men can consider by the Penn the aucthoritie of the writer, thoughe they know him not. The Rubie is discerned by his pale rednes, and who hath not h[e]ard that the Lyon is knowne by hys clawes. Though *Æsopes* craftie crowe be never so deftlye decked, yet is his double dealing e[a]sely desiphered: and though men never so perfectly pollish there wrytings with others sentences, yet the simple truth wil discover the shadow of ther follies: and bestowing every fether in the bodye of the right M. tourne out the naked dissembler into his owen cote, as a spectacle of follye to all those which can rightlye judge what imperfections be.

There came to my hands lately a litle (woulde God a wittye) pamphelet, baring a fayre face as though it were the sc[h]oole of abuse, but being by me advisedly wayed I fynd it the oftscome of imperfections, the writer fuller of wordes than judgement; the matter certainely as ridiculus as seri[o]us. Asuredly his mother witte wrought this wonder, the child to disprayse his father, the dogg to byte his mayster for his dainty morcell. But I se[e] (with *Seneca*) yt the[Pg 3] wrong is to be suffered, since he disprayseth, who by costome hath left to speake well; bot I meane to be short: and teach the Maister what he knoweth not, partly that he may se his owne follie, and partly that I may discharge my promise, both binde me. Therefore I would with the good scholmayster to over looke his abuses againe with me, so shall he see an ocean of inormities which begin in his first prinsiple in the disprayse of poetry.

And first let me familiarly consider with this find faulte what the learned have alwayes esteemed of poetrie. *Seneca* thoughe a stoike would have a poeticall sonne, and amongst the auncientest *Homer* was no les accompted than *Humanus deus*. What made Alexander I pray you esteme of him so much? Why allotted he for his works so curious a closset? Was ther no fitter under prop for his pillow the[n] a simple pamphelet? In all *Darius* cofers was there no Jewell so costly? Forso[o]th my thinks these two (the one the father of Philosophers, the other the cheftaine of chivalrie) were both deceived if all were as a *Gosson* would wish them, yf poets paynt naughte but palterie toyes in vearse, their studies tended to folishnesse, and in all their inde[a]vors they did naught els but *agendo nihil agere*. Lord how Virgil's poore gnatt pricketh him, and how Ovid's fley byteth him, he can beare no bourde, he hath raysed up a new sect of seri[o]us stoikes, that can abide naught[Pg 4] but their owen shadowe, and alow nothing worthye, but what they conceave. Did you never reade (my over wittie frend) that under the persons of beastes many abuses were dissiphered? Have you not reason to waye? that whatsoever e[i]ther Virgil did write of his gnatt, or Ovid of his fley, was all covertly to declare abuse? But you are (*homo literatus*) a man of the letter, little savoring of learning, your giddy brain made you leave your thrift, and your abuses in London some part of your honestie. You say that Poets are subtil, if so, you have learned that poynt of them, you can well glose on a trifleling text: but you have dronke perhaps of *Lethe*, your gram[m]er learning is out of your head, you forget your Accidence, you reme[m]ber not that under the person of *Æneas* in Virgil, the practice of a dilligent captaine is discribed, under ye shadow of byrds, beastes, and trees, the follies of the world were disiphered, you know not that the creation is signified in the Image of *Prometheus*, the fall of pryde in the person of *Narcissus*, these are toyes because they savour of wisedom which you want. Marke what *Campanus* sayth, *Mira fabularum vanitas sed quæ si introspiciantur videri possunt non vanæ*. The vanitie of tales is wonderful, yet if we advisedly looke into them they wil seme and prove wise. How wonderful are the pithie poems of *Cato*! the curious comidies of *Plautus*! how bravely discovereth *Terence* our imperfectio[n] in his *Eunuch*![Pg 5] how neatly dissiphereth he *Dauus*! how pleasauntly paynteth he out *Gnatho*! whom if we should seeke in our dayes, I suppose he would not be farr from your parson. But I see you woulde seeme to be that which you are not, and as the proverb sayth *Nodum in Cirpo quærere*. Poets you say use coullors to cover their incoviences, and wittie sentences to burnish theyr bawdery, and you divinite to cover your knaverye.

But tell mee truth *Gosson*, speakest thou as thou thinkest? What coelers findest thou in a Poete not to be admitted? Are his speaches unperfect? Savor they of inscience? I think if thou hast any shame thou canst not but like and approve the[m]. Are ther gods displesant unto thee? doth *Saturne* in his majesty move thee? doth *Juno* with her riches displease thee? doth *Minerva* with her weapon discomfort thee? doth *Apollo* with his harping harme thee? Thou mayst say nothing les then harme thee because they are not, and I thinke so to[o] because thou knowest them not. For wot thou that in the person of *Saturne* our decaying yearss are signified, in the picture of angry *Juno* our affections are dissiphered, in ye person of *Minerva* is our understa[n]ding signified, both in respect of warre, as policie. When they faine that *Pallas* was begotten of the braine of *Jupiter* their meaning is none other but that al wisdome (as the learned say) is from above, and commeth from the father of Lights: in the portrature of *Apollo* all[Pg 6] knowledge is denocated. So that, what so they wrot it was to this purpose, in the way of pleasure to draw men to wisedome: for se[e]ing the world in those daies was unperfect, yt was necessary that they like good Phisi[ci]ons should so frame their potions, that they might be appliable to the quesie stomaks of their werish patients. But our studientes by your meanes have made shipwrack of theyr labors, our schoole-maisters have so offended that by your judgement they shall *subire pœnam capitis* for teaching poetry, the universitie is litle beholding to you, al their practices in teaching are frivolus. Witt hath wrought that in you, that yeares and studie never set[t]led in the heads of our sagest doctors.

No mervel though you disprayse poetrye, when you know not what it meanes. *Erasmus* will make that the pathwaye to knowledge which you disprayse, and no meane fathers vouchsafe in their seriouse questions of divinitie, to inserte poeticall sensures.

I think if we shal wel overloke ye Philosophers, we shal find their judgeme[n]ts not halfe perfect. Poetes you say fayle in their fables, Philosophers in the verye secrets of Nature. Though *Plato* could wish the expulsion of Poetes from his well publiques, which he might doe with reason, yet the wisest had not all that same opinion, it had bene better for him to have se[a]rcht more narowly what the soule was, for his definition was verye frivolus, when he would make[Pg 7] it naught els but *Substantiam intelectu predictam*. If you say that Poetes did labour about nothing, tell me (I besech you) what wonders wroughte those your dunce Doctors in ther reasons *de ente et non ente*, in theyr definition of no force and les witt? How sweate they power soules in makinge more things then co[u]ld be! That I may use your owne phrase, did not they spende one candle by seeking another? *Democritus Epicurus* with ther scholler *Metrodorus* how labored they in finding out more worlds the[n] one? Your *Plato* in midst of his presisnes wrought that absurdite that never may be redd in Poets, to make a yearthly creature to beare the person of the creator, and a corruptible substaunce an incomprehensible God: for determining of the principall causes of all thinges, a made them naughte els but an *Idea* which if it be conferred wyth the truth, his sentence will savour of Inscience. But I speake for Poetes, I answeare your abuse, therefore I will disprove or disprayse naught, but wish you with the wise *Plato*, to disprayse that thing you offend not in.

Seneca sayth that the studdie of Poets is to make childre[n] ready to the understanding of wisedom, and yt our auncients did teache *artes Eleutherias. i. liberales*, because the instructed childre[n] by the instrume[n]t of knowledg in time became *homines liberi. i. Philosophye*. It may be that in reding of poetry, it happened to you as it is with the Oyster, for she in her swimming receiveth no ayre, and you in your reeding lesse instruction. It is reported that the shepe of Euboia want ther gale, and one the contrarye side that the beastes of *Naxus* have *distentum fel*. Men hope that scollers should have witt brought upp in the Universite, but your sweet selfe with the cattell of Euboia, since you left your College have lost your learning. You disprayse *Maximinus Tirius* pollicey, and that thinge that he wrott to manifest learned Poets meaning, you atribute to follye. O holy hedded man, why may not *Juno* resemble the ayre? why not *Alexander* valour? why not *Ulisses* pollice? Will you have all for you[r] owne tothe? Must men write that you maye know theyr meaning as though your wytt were to wrest all things? Alas simple *Irus*, begg at knowledge gate awhile, thou haste not wonne the mastery of learning. Weane thyself to wisedome, and use thy tallant in zeale not for envie, abuse not thy knowledge in dispraysing that which is pereles: I shold blush from a player, to become an enviouse preacher, if thou hadst zeale to preach, if for *Sions* sake thou co[u]ldst not holde thy tongue, thy true dealing were prayse worthy, thy revolting woulde counsell me to reverence thee. Pittie weare it that poetrye should be displaced, full little could we want *Buchanan's* workes, and *Boetius* comfortes may not be banished. What made *Erasmus* labor in *Euripides* tragedies? Did he inde[a]vour by painting them out of Greeke into Latine to manifest sinne unto us, or to confirm us in goodnes? Labor (I pray thee) in Pamphelets more prayse worthy; thou haste not saved a Senator, therefore not worthye a Lawrell wre[a]th, thou hast not (in disproving poetry) reproved an abuse, and therfore not worthy commendation.

Seneca sayth that *Magna vitæ pars elabitur male agentibus, maxima nihill agentibus, tota aliud agentibus*, the most of our life (sayd he) is spent e[i]ther in doing evill, or nothing, or that wee should not, and I would wish you weare exempted from this sensure. Geve eare but a little more what may be said for poetrie, for I must be briefe. You have made so greate matter that I may not stay on one thing to[o] long, lest I leave another untouched.

And first whereas you say, yt *Tullie* in his yeres of more judgement despised Poetes, harke (I pray you) what he worketh for them in his oratio[n] *pro Archia poeta*. But before you heare him, least you fayle in the incounter, I would wysh you to follow the advise of the dasterdlye Ichneumon of *Ægipt*, who when shee beholdeth the Aspis her enemye to drawe nighe, calleth her fellowes together, bisme[a]ring herselfe with claye, against the byting and stroke of the serpent, arme yourselfe, cal your witts together: want not your wepons, lest your inperfect judgement be rewardede with Midas eares. You had neede play the night burd now, for yon day Owl hath[Pg 10] misconned his parte, and for to-who now a dayes he cryes foole you: which hath brought such a sort of wondering birds about your eares, as I feare me will chatter you out of your Ivey bush. The worlde shames to see you, or els you are afrayde to shew yourselfe.

You thought poetrye should want a patron (I think) when you fyrste published this invective, but yet you fynd al to[o] many eve[n] *preter expectationē*, yea though it can speake for it self, yet her patron *Tullie* now shall tell her tale, *Hæc studia*, (sayth he) *adolescentiam alunt, senectutem oblectant, secundas res ornant, adversis perfugium ac Solatium prebent, delectant domi, non impediunt foris, pernoctant nobiscum, peregri[n]antur rusticantur*. Then will you disprayse yt which all men commend? You looke only upon ye refuse of ye abuse, nether respecting the importance of ye matter nor the weighe of ye wryter.

Solon can fayne himself madde, to further the Athenians. *Chaucer* in pleasant vain can rebuke sin uncontrold, and though he be lavish in the letter, his sence is serious. Who in Rome lame[n]ted not Roscius death? And ca[n]st thou suck no plesure out of thy *M. Claudians* writings? Hark what *Cellarius* a learned father attributed to it, *acuit memoriam* (saith he) it profiteth the memory. Yea, and *Tully* attributeth it for prais to *Archias* yt upon any theame he co[u]ld versify exte[m]pory. Who liketh not of the promptness of *Ovid*? Who not unworthely[Pg 11] co[u]ld boast of himself thus *Quicquid conabar dicere versus erat*. Who then doothe not wonder at poetry? Who thinketh not yt it procedeth fro[m] above? What made ye Chians and Colophonians fal to such controversy? Why seke ye Smirnians to recover fro[m] ye Salaminians the prais of *Homer*? Al wold have him to be of ther city, I hope not for harme, but because of his knoledge. *Themistocles* desireth to be acquainted with those w^c could best discipher his praises. Even *Marius* himselfe, tho never so cruel, acco[m]pted of *Plotinus* poems. What made *Aphricanus* esteme *Ennius*? Why did Alexander give prais to *Achilles* but for ye prayses which he found writte[n] of hym by *Homer*? Why estemed *Pompie* so muche of *Theophanes Mitiletus*, or *Brutus* so greatlye the wrytinges of *Accius*? *Fuluius* was so great a favorer of poetry, that after the Aetolian warres, he attributed to the Muses those spoiles that belonged to Mars. In all the Romaine conquest, h[e]ardest thou ever of a slayne Poete? nay rather the Emperours honored them, beautified them with benefites, and decked their sanctuaries which [with] sacrifice. *Pindarus* colledg is not fit for spoil of *Alexander* overcome, nether feareth poetry ye persecutors sword. What made *Austin* so much affectate ye heavenly fury? not folly, for if I must needes speake, *illud non ausim affirmare*, his zeale was in setting up the house of God, not in affectate[Pg 12] eloquence, he wrot not, he accompted not. He honnored not, so much that (famous poetry) whyche we prayse, without cause, for if it be true that *Horace* reporteth in his booke *de arte poetica,* all the answeares of the

Oracles weare in verse. Among the precise Jewes you shall find Poetes, and for more majestie *Sibilla* will prophesie in verse. *Hiroaldus* can witnes with me, that *David* was a poet, and that his vayne was in imitating (as S. Jerom witnesseth) *Horace, Flaccus,* and *Pindarus,* somtimes his verse runneth in an *Iambus* foote, anone he hath recourse to a *Saphier* vaine, and *aliquando, semipede ingreditur.* Ask *Josephus,* and he will tel you that Esay, Job and Salomon voutsafed poetical practises, for (if *Origen* and he fault not) theyre verse was *Hexameter and pentameter.* Enquire of *Cassiodorus,* he will say that all the beginning of Poetrye proceeded from the Scripture. *Paulinus* tho the byshop of *Nolanum* yet voutsafe the name of a Poet, and *Ambrose* tho he be a patriarke in *mediolanū* loveth versising. *Beda* shameth not ye science that shamelesse *Gosson* misliketh. Reade over *Lactantius,* his proofe is by poetry, and *Paul* voutsafeth to overlooke *Epimenides*; let the Apostle preach at Athens he disdaineth not of Aratus authorite. It is a pretye sentence yet not so prety as pithy, *Poeta nascitur orator fit*, as who should say, Poetrye commeth from above from a heavenly seate of a glorious God unto[Pg 13] an excellent creature man, an orator is but made by exercise. For if wee examine well what befell *Ennius* amonge the Romans, and Hesiodus among his co[u]ntrimen the Gretians, howe they came by theyr knowledge whence they receved their heavenly furye, the first will tell us that sleping upon the Mount of Parnassus he dreamed that he received the soule of *Homer* into him, after the which he became a Poete, the next will assure you that it commeth not by labor, nether that night watchings bringeth it, but yt we must have it thence whence he fetched it w^c was (he saith) fro[m] a wel of ye Muses w^c *Cabelimus* calleth *Porū*, a draught whereof drewe him to his perfection, so of a shephard he becam an eloque[n]t poet.

Wel the[n] you see yt it commeth not by exercise of play making, nether insertio[n] of gawds, but from nature and from above: and I hope yt *Aristotle* hath sufficiently taught you that *Natura nihil fecit frustra.*

Perseus was made a poete *divino furore percitus*. And whereas the poets were sayde to call for the Muses helpe ther mening was no other as *Iodocus Badius* reporteth, but to call for heavenly inspiration from above to direct theyr ende[a]vors. Nether were it good for you to sette light by the name of a poet since ye oftspring from whence he cometh is so heavenly. *Sibilla* in hir answers to *Æneas* against hir will as the poet telleth us was possessed with[Pg 14] thys fury, ye wey consideratly but of the writing of poets, and you shal se[e] than whe[n] ther matter is most heavenly, their stile is most loftye, a strange token of the wonderfull efficacy of the same.

I would make a long discourse unto you of *Platos* 4. furies but I le[a]ve them. It pitieth me to bring a rodd of your owne making to beate you wythal. But mithinks while you heare thys I see you swallowe down your owne spittle for revenge, where (God wot) my wryting savoreth not of envye. In this case I coulde wyshe you fare farre otherwyse from your foe. If you please I wyll become your frende and see what a potion or receypt I can frame fytt for your diet. And herein I will prove myselfe a practiser, before I purdge you, you shall take a preparative to disburden your heavy hedde of those grose follis you have conceved: but the receipt is bitter, therefore I would wysh you first to casten your mouth with the Suger of persevera[n]ce: for ther is a cold collop yt must downe your throate yet suche a one as shall change your complection quit[e]. I wyll have you therfore to tast first of yt cold river *Phricus* in Thratia, which as *Aristotle* reporteth changeth blacke into white; or of Scamandar, which maketh gray yalow, yt is of an envious ma[n] a wel minded person, reprehending of zeale yt wherin he hath sinned by folly, and so being prepard, thy purgation wyll worke more easy, thy understandinge wyll be[Pg 15] more perfit, thou shalt blush at thy abuse, and reclaime thy selfe by force of argument. So will thou prove of clene recovered patient, and I a perfecte practiser in framing so good a potion. This broughte to passe, I with the[e] wil seeke out some abuse in poetry, which I will seeke for to disprove by reason first pronounced by no smal birde even *Aristotle* himself.

Poetae (sayth he) *multa mentiuntur* and to further his opinion seuer *Cato* putteth in his cencure.

Admiranda canunt sed non credenda poetæ. These were sore blemishes if objected rightly and heare you may say the streme runnes a wronge, but if it be so by you[r] leve I wyll bring him shortly in his right chanel. My answere shall not be my owne, but a learned father shall tell my tale, if you wil know his right name men call him *Lactantius*: who in hys book *de divinis institutionibus* reesoneth thus. I suppose (sayth he) Poets are full of credit, and yet it is requesite for those that wil understand them to be admonished, that among them not onely the name but the matter beareth a show of that it is not: for if sayth he we examine the Scriptures litterallye nothing will seeme more falls, and if we way Poetes wordes and not ther meaning, our learning in them wilbe very mene. You see nowe your *Catoes* judgement as of no force and that all your objections you make agaynst poetrye be of no valor, yet lest you[Pg 16] should be altogether discouraged I wyll helpe you forwarde a little more, it pities me to consider the weaknes of your cause, I wyll therfore make your strongest reason more strong and after I have builded it up destroy it agayn. Poets you confesse are eloquent but you reprove them in their wantonnesse, they write of no wisedom, you may say their tales are frivolus, they prophane holy thinges, they seeke nothing to the perfection of our soules. Theyr practise is in other things of lesse force: to this objection I answer no otherwise then *Horace* doeth in his booke *de arte poetica* where he wryteth thus:

Silvestres homines sacer interpresque deorum
Sedibus, et victu fœdo deterruit orpheus.
Dictus ob hoc lenire Tigres rabidosque leones.
Dictus et Amphion Thebanæ condit[or] urbis
Saxa movere sono, testudinis et prece blanda
Ducere quo vellet. Fuit hoc sapientia quondam,
Publica privatis secernere sacra prophanis,
Concubitu prohibere vago, dare Iura maritis,
Oppida moliri, leges incidere ligno.

The holy spokesman of the Gods
With heave[n]ly Orpheus hight:
Did drive the savage men from wods,
And made them live aright.
And therefore is sayd the Tygers fierce,
And Lyons full of myght
To overcome: *Amphion*, he
Was sayd of Theabs the founder,
[Pg 17] Who by his force of Lute dyd cause
The stones to part a sonder,
And by his speach did them derect
Where he would have them staye:
This wisedome this was it of olde
All strife for to allaye.
To give to every man his owne,
To make the Gods be knowne,
To drive each lecher from the bed
That never was his owne.
To teach the law of mariage,
The way to build a towne,
For to engrave these lawes in woods
This was these mens renowne.

I cannot leave *Tirtheus* pollicy untouched, who by force of his pen could incite men to the defence of theyr countrye. If you require of ye Oracle of *Apollo* what successe you shal have: *respondet bellicoso numine*. Lo now you see your objections my answers, you behold or may perceive manifestlye that Poetes was the first raysors of cities, prescribers of good lawes, mayntayners of religion, disturbors of the wicked, advancers of the wel disposed, inve[n]tors of laws, and lastly the very fo[o]tpaths to knowledg and understa[n]ding. Ye if we sho[u]ld beleve Herome he will make *Platos* exiles honest me[n] and his pestiferous poets good preachers: for he accounteth *Orpheus Museus and Linus, Christians*, therefore *Virgil* (in his 6 boke of *Æneiados* wher he lernedly describeth ye journey of *Æneas* to *Elisum*) asserteneth[Pg 18] us, yt among them yt were ther for the zeale they beare toward there country, ther wer found *Quinque pii vates et Phœbo digna loquti* but I must answer al objectio[n]s, I must fil every nooke. I must arme myself now, for here is the greatest bob I can gather out of your booke forsoth *Ovids* abuses, in descrybing whereof you labour very vehementlye termi[n]g him letcher, and in his person dispraise all poems, but shall on[e] mans follye destroye a universal comodity? What gift what perfit knowledg hath ther bin, emong ye professors of w^c ther hath not bin a bad on [?] the Angels have sinned in heave[n], *Ada[m] and Eve* in earthly paradise, emo[n]g ye holy apostles ungratious Judas. I reson not yt al poets are holy but I affirme yt poetry is a heave[n]ly gift, a perfit gift then which I know not greater plesure. And surely if I may speak my mind I thi[n]k we shall find but few poets if it were exactly wayd what they oughte to be: your *Muscovian* straungers, your *Scithian* monsters wonderful, by one *Eurus* brought upon one stage in ships made of Sheepeskins, wyll not prove you a poet nether your life alow you to bee of that learning: if you had wisely wayed ye abuse of poetry, if you had reprehended ye foolish fantasies of our poets *nomine non re* which they bring forth on stage, my self would have liked of you and allowed your labor. But I perceive nowe yt all red colloured stones are not Rubies, nether is every one *Alexandar*[Pg 19] yt hath a stare in his cheeke, al lame men are not *Vulcans*, nor hooke nosed men *Ciceroes*, nether each professer a poet, I abhore those poets that savor of ribaldry, I will with the zealous admit the expullcion of suche enormities. Poetry is dispraised not for the folly that is in it, but for the abuse whiche manye ill Wryters couller by it. Beleeve me the magestrats may take advise (as I knowe wisely can) to roote out those odd rymes which runnes in every rascales mouth. Savoring of rybaldry, those foolishe ballets that are admitted make poets good and godly practises to be refused. I like not of a wicked *Nero* that wyll expell *Lucan*, yet admit I of a zealous governour that wil seke to take away the abuse of poetry. I like not of an angrye *Augustus* which wyll banishe *Ovid* for envy. I love a wise Senator, which in wisedome wyll correct him and with advise burne his follyes:

unhappy were we yf like poore *Scaurus* we shoulde find *Tiberius* that wyll put us to death for a tragedy making, but most blessed were we if we might find a judge that severely would amende the abuses of Tragedies. But I leave the reformation thereof to more wyser than my selfe, and retourne to Gosson whom I wyshe to be fully perswaded in this cause, and therefore I will tell hym a prety story, which *Justin* wryteth in the prayse of poetrye.

The *Lacedemonians* when they had loste many men in divers incountryes with theyr enemyes soughte[Pg 20] to the Oracles of Apollo requiring how they myght recover theyr losses, it was answered that they mighte overcome if so be they could get an *Athenian* governor, whereupon they sent Orators unto the *Athenians* humbly requesting them that they woulde appoynt them out one of theyr best captaynes: the *Athenians* owinge them old malice, sent them in steede of a *soldado vechio* a scholar of the Muses: in steede of a worthy warrior a poore poet; for a couragious *Themistocles* a silly *Tirthetus*, a man of great eloquence and singuler wytte, yet was he but a lame lymde captaine more fit for the co[u]che than the field. The *Lacedemonians* trusting the Oracle, received the champion, and fearing the government of a stranger, made him ther Citizen. Which once done and he obteining the Dukdome, he assended the theater, and ther very learnedly, wyshing them to forget theyr folly, and to thinke on victory, they being acuate by his eloque[n]ce waging battail won the fielde. Lo now you see that the framing of common welthes, and defence thereof proceedeth from poets, how dare you therfore open your mouth against them? How can you disprayse the preserver of a countrye? You compare *Homer* to *Methecus*, cookes to Poetes, you shame your selfe in your unreverent similitud[e]s, you may see your follyes *verbum sapienti sat*: whereas *Homar* was an ancient poet you disalow him, and accompte of those of lesser judgement. *Strabo* calleth[Pg 21] poetry *primam sapientiam*. Cicero in his firste of his Tusculans attributeth ye invencion of philosophy to poets. God keepe us from a Plato that should expel such men. Pittie were it that the memory of these valiant victours should be hidden, which have dyed in the behalfe of ther countryes: miserable were our state yf we wanted those worthy volumes of poetry. Could the learned beare the losse of Homer? or our younglings the wrytings of the *Mantuan*? or you your volumes of historyes? beleve me yf you had wanted your Mysteries of nature, and your stately storyes, your booke would have scarce bene ledde wyth matter. If therefore you will deale in things of wisdome, correct the abuse, honor the science, renewe your schoole, crye out over Hierusalem wyth the prophet the woe that he pronounced, wish the teacher to reforme hys lyfe, that his weake scholler may prove the wyser, cry out against unsaciable desyre in rich men, tel the house of Jacob theyr iniquities, lament with the Apostle the want of laborers in the Lords vineyards, cry out on those dume doggs that will not barke, wyll the mightye that they overmayster not the poore, and put downe the beggers prowde heart by thy perswasions. Thunder oute with the Prophete *Micha* the mesage of the LORD, and with hym desyre the Judges to heare thee, the Prynces of Jacob to hearken to thee, and those of the house of Israell to understande. Then tell them that they abhorre[Pg 22] judgement, and prevent equitie, that they judge for rewardes, and that theyr priests teach for hyre, and the prophets thereof prophesie for money, and yet that they saye the Lorde is wyth them, and that no evil can befall them, breath[e] out the sweete promises to the good, the cursses to the badde, tell them that a peeace muste needes have a warre, and that God can raise up another Zenacherib, shew the[m] that Salomons kingdome was but for a season and that adversitie cometh ere we espye it. These be the songes of Sion, these be those rebukes which you oughte to add to abuses; recover the body for it is sore, the appedices thereof will easily be reformed, if that wear at a staye.

But other matters call me and I must not staye upon this onely, there is an easier task in hand for me, and that which, if I may speak my conscience, fitteth my vain best, your second abuse Gosson, your second abuse; your disprayses of Musik, which you unadvisedly terme pyping: that is it will most byte you, what so is a overstay of life, is displesant to your person, musik may not stand in your presence, whereas all the learned Philosophers have alwayes had it in reverence. *Homar* commendeth it highly, referring to the prayses of the Gods whiche Gosson accompteth folishnesse; looke uppon the harmonie of the Heavens; hang they not by Musik? Doe not the *Spheares* move? The *primus* motor governe[s], be not[Pg 23] they *inferiora corpora* affected *quadam sumpathia* and agreement? Howe can we measure the debilitie of the patient but by the disordered motion of the pulse? Is not man worse accompted of when he is most out of tune? Is there any thinge that more affecteth the sense? Doth there any pleasure more acuat our understanding? Can the wonders yt hath wroughte and which you your selfe confesse no more move you? It fitteth well nowe that the learned have sayd, *musica requirit generosum animu[m]* which since it is far from you, no marvel though you favor not that profession. It is reported of the *Camelion* that shee can chaunge her selfe unto all coollors save whyte, and you can accompte of all thinges save such as have honesty. *Plutarch* your good Mayster may bare me witness that the ende whereto Musick was, will proove it prayes worthy. O Lord howe maketh it a man to remember heavenly things to wo[n]der at the works of the creator. *Eloquence* can stay the souldiars sworde from slayinge an Orator, and shall not musike be magnified which not onely saveth the bodye but is a comfort to the soule? David rejoyseth singeth and prayeth the Lorde by the Harpe, and the Simbale is not removed from his sanctuary, the Aungels syng *gloria in excelsis*. Surely the imagination in this present instant calleth me to a deepe consideration of my God. Looke for wonders where musike worketh, and wher harmonie is ther followeth[Pg 24] increcible delectation. The bowels of the earth y[i]eld where the instrument soundeth and *Pluto* cannot keepe *Proserpina* if *Orpheus* recorde. The Seas shall not swallowe *Arion* whilst he singeth, nether shall hee perish while he harpeth, a doleful tuner yf a diing musition can move a Monster of ye sea to mourne. A Dolphin respectet a heavenly recorde.

Call your selfe home therefore and reclayme thys follye, it is to[o] foule to bee admitted, you may not mayntaine it. I hadd well hoped you woulde in all these thynges have wiselye admytted the thyng, and disalowe naughte but the abus, but I see your mynde in youre wrytinge was to penn somewhat you knowe not what, and to confyrme it I wot not howe, so that yourselfe hath hatched us an Egge yet so that it hath blest us wyth a monsterus chickin, both wythoute hedde, and also tayle, lyke the Father, full of imperfection and lesse zeale. Well marke yet a lyttle more, beare with me though I be bytter, my love is never the lesse for that I have learned of *Tullye*, that *Nulla remedia tam faciunt dolorem quam quæ sunt salutaria*, the sharper medycine the better it cures, the more you see your follye, the sooner may you amend it. Are not the straines in Musike to tickle and delyght the eare? are not our warlike instruments to move men to valor? you confesse they moove us, but yet they delight not our eares? I pray you whence grew that poynt of Phylosophy? It is more then[Pg 25] ever my Mayster taught mee, that a thynge of sounde shoulde not delyghte the eare. Belyke yee suppose that men are monsters, withoute eares, or else I thynke you wyll saye they heare with theire heeles, it may bee so; for indeede when wee are delighted with Musike, it maketh our heart to scypp for joye, and it maye bee perhaps by assending from the heele to the hygher partes, it may move us, good policie in sooth, this was of your owne coyning, your mother never taught it you, but I wyll not deale by reason of philosophye wyth you for that confound your senses, but I can asure you this one thinge, that this principle will make the wiser to mislike your invention, it had bene a fitter jest for your howlet in your playe, then an orname[n]t in your booke. But since you wrote of abuses, we may licence you to lye a little, so ye abuse will be more manifest. Lord with how goodly a cote have you clothed your conceiptes, you abound in storyes but impertinent, they bewray your reeding but not your wisedom, would God they had bin well aplyed. But now I must play the musitian right nolesse buggs now come in place but pavions and mesures, dumps and fancies, and here growes a great question what musick *Homer* used in curing ye diseased gretians, it was no dump you say, and so think I, for yt is not apliable to sick men, for it favoreth Malancholie. I am sure it was no mesure, for in those days they were not such good da[n]sers,[Pg 26] for so[o]th the[n] what was it? If you require me, if you name me the instrume[n]t, I wyl tel you what was ye musik. Meanwhile a gods name let us both dout yt is no part of our salvation to know what it was nor how it went. When I speak with *Homer* next you shall knowe his answere.

But you can not be content to erre but you must maintain it to[o]. *Pithagoras* you say alowes not that musik is decerned by eares, but hee wisheth us to assend unto the sky and marke that harmony. Surely this is but one doctors opinion (yet I dislike not of it) but to speake my conscience my thinkes musike best pleaseth me when I heare it, for otherwise the catter walling of Cats, were it not for harmonie, should more delight mine eies then the tunable voyces of men. But these things are not the chiefest poynts you shote at, thers somewhat els sticketh in your stomak God graunt it hurt you not, from the daunce you runn to the pype from 7. to 3. which if I shoulde add I beleeve I could wrest out halfe a score inco[n]veniences more out of your booke. Our pleasant consortes do discomfort you much, and because you lyke not thereof they arr discomendable, I have heard it is good to take sure fotinge when we travel unknowen countryes, for when we wade above our shoe latchet *Appelles* wyll reprehende us for coblers, if you had bene a father in musick and coulde have decerned of tunes I would perhaps have likt[Pg 27] your opinion sumwhat where now I abhor it, if you wear a professor of that practise I would quickly perswade you, that the adding of strings to our instrument make the sound more hermonious, and that the mixture of Musike maketh a better concent. But to preach to unskillfull is to perswad ye brut beastes, I wyl not stand long in thys point although the dignitye thereof require a volume, but howe learned men have esteemed this heavenly gift, if you please to read you shall see. *Socrates* in hys old age will not disdain to learn ye science of Music amo[n]g children, he can abide their correctio[n]s to[o], so much accou[n]ted he that wt you contemn, so profitable thought he yt, wt you mislik. *Solon* wil esteme so much of ye knowledg of singing, yt he wil soner forget to dye the[n] to sing. *Pithagoras* liks it so wel yt he wil place it in *Greace*, and *Aristoxenus* will saye yt the soule is musik. *Plato* (in his booke *de legibus*) will affirme that it can not be handled without all sciences, the *Lacedemonians and Cretensis* wer sturred to warre by Anapæstus foote, and *Timotheus* with the same incensed kinge *Alexander* to batel, ye yf *Boetyus* fitten not, on *Tauromitanus* (by this *Phrigian* sound) hastened to burn a house wher a stru[m]pet was hidden.

So little abideth this heave[n]ly harmony our humane filthines yt it worketh wonders as you may perceve most manifestly by the history of *Agamemnon*[Pg 28] who going to ye Trojan war, left at home a musitian yt playde the *Dorian* tune, who wt the foote *Spondeus* preserved his wife *Clitemnestra* in chastity and honesty, wherfore she co[u]ld not be deflowred by *Ægistus*, before he had wickedly slain the musitian. So yt as the magnetes draweth Iorne, and the Theamides (w^c groweth in *Ægipt*) driveth it away: so musik calleth to it selfe al honest plesures, and dispelleth fro[m] it all vaine misdemanors. Yt matter is so ple[n]tiful that I cannot find wher to end, as for beginnings they be infinite, but these shall suffice. I like not to[o] long circu[m]stances wher les doe serve: only I wish you to accompt wel of this heave[n]ly concent, w^c is ful of perfettio[n], preceding fro[m] above, drawing his original fro[m] the motion of ye stars, fro[m] the agrement of the planets, fro[m] the whisteling winds, and fro[m] al those celestial circles where is e[i]ther perfit agreeme[n]t or any *Sumphonia*. But as I like musik so admit I not of thos that deprave the same: your pipers are as odius to mee as yourselfe; nether alowe I your harpinge merye beggers: although I knewe you my selfe a professed play maker, and a paltry actor. Since which ye windmil of your wit hath bin tornd so long wyth the wynde of folly, that I fear me we shall see the dogg returne to his vomit, and the clensed sow to her myre, and the reformed scholemayster to hys old teaching of follye. Beware it be not so, let not your booke be[Pg 29] a blemish to your own profession. Correct not musik therfore whe[n] it is praiesworthy, least your worthlesse misliking bewray your madnes. Way the abuse and that is matter sufficient to serve a magistrates animadversion. Heere may you advise well, and if you have any stale rethorik florish upon thys text, the abuse is, when that is applyed to wantonnesse, which was created to shewe Gods worthinesse. When ye shamefull resorts of shameles curtezanes in sinful sonnets shall prophane vertue, these are no light sinnes, these make many good men lament, this causeth parents hate there right borne children, if this were reformed by your policie I should esteme of you as you wysh. I feare me it fareth far otherwyse, *latet anguis in herba*, under your fare show of conscience take heede you cloake not your abuse, it were pittie the learned should be overseene in your simplenesse, I feare me you will be politick wyth *Machavel* not zealous as a prophet. Well I will not stay long upon the abuse, for that I see it is to[o] manifest, the remembraunce thereof is discommendable among the godly, and I my self am very loth to bring it in memory. To the wise advised reader these mai suffice, to flee the *Crocodel* before he commeth, lest we be bitten, and to avoyde the abuse of musik, since we se[e] it, lest our misery be more when we fall into folly. *Ictus piscator sapit*, you heare open confession, these abuses are disclaimed by our Gosson, he is sory [Pg 30] that hee hath so leudlye lived, and spent the oyle of his perfection in unsavery Lampes. He hath *Argus* eyes to watch him now, I wold wish him beware of his Islington, and such lyke resorts, if now he retourne from his repented lyfe to his old folly, Lord how foule will be his fall. Men know more then they speak if they be wise, I feare me some will blush that readeth this, if he be bitten, wold God Gosson at that instant might have a watchman. But I see it were needelesse, perhaps he hath *Os durum*, and then what avayleth their presence.

Well, I leave this poynt til I know further of your mynde, mean while I must talke a little wyth you about ye thyrd abuse, for the cater cosens of pypers, theyr names (as you terme them) be players, and I think as you doe, for your experience is sufficient to enforme me. But here I must loke about me, *quacunque tetigeris ulcus est*, here is a task that requireth a long treatis, and what my opinion is of players ye now shall plainly perceve. I must now serch my wits, I see this shall passe throughe many severe sensors handling, I must advise me what I write, and write that I would wysh. I way wel the seriousnes of the cause, and regarde very much the Judges of my endevor, whom if I could I would perswade that I woulde not nourish abuse, nether mayntaine that which should be an universall discomoditye. I hope they wil not judge before they [Pg 31] read, nether condemne without occasion. The wisest wil alwais carry to eares, in yt they are to diserne two indifferent causes. I meane not to hold you in suspe[n]c[e] (severe Judges) if you gredely expect my verdit brefely this it is.

Demostines thoughte not that *Phillip* shoulde overcome when he reproved hym, nether feared *Cicero Anthonies* force when in the Senatt hee rebuked hym. To the ignorant e[a]ch thinge that is unknowne semes unprofitable, but a wise man can foresee and prayse by proofe. *Pythagoras* could spy oute in womens eyes two kind of teares, the one of grefe the other of disceit: and those of judgement can from the same flower suck honey with the bee, from whence the Spyder (I mean the ignorant) take their poison. Men yt have knowledge what comedies and tragedis be, wil comend the[m], but it is sufferable in the folish to reprove that they know not, becaus ther mouthes wil hardly be stopped. Firste therfore, if it be not tedious to Gosson to harken to the lerned, the reder shall perceive the antiquity of playmaking, the inventors of comedies, and therewithall the use and comoditaye of the[m]. So that in ye end I hope my labor shall be liked, and the learned wil soner conceve his folly.

For tragedies and comedies *Donate* the gramarian sayth, they wer invented by lerned fathers of the old time to no other purpose, but to yeelde prayse unto [Pg 32] God for a happy harvest, or plentifull yeere, and that thys is trewe the name of Tragedye doeth importe, for if you consider whence it came, you shall perceive (as *Iodocus Badius* reporteth) that it drewe his original of *Tragos, Hircus*, and *Ode, Cantus* (so called), for that the actors thereof had in rewarde for theyr labour, a Gotes skynne fylled wyth wyne. You see then that the fyrste matter of tragedies was to give thankes and prayses to GOD, and a gratefull prayer of the countrymen for a happye harvest, and this I hope was not discommendable. I knowe you will judge [th]is farthest from abuse. But to wade farther, thys fourme of invention being found out, as the dayes wherein it was used did decay, and the world grew to more perfection, so yt witt of the younger sorte became more riper, for they leaving this fourme, invented an other, in the which they altered the nature but not ye name: for sounets in prayse of ye gods, they did set forth the sower fortune of many exiles, the miserable fal of haples princes, the reuinous decay of many cou[n]tryes, yet not content with this, they presented the lives of *Satyers*, so that they might wiselye, under the abuse of that name, discover the follies of many theyr folish fellow-citesens: and those monsters were then, as our parasites are now adayes: suche as with pleasure reprehended abuse. As for commedies because they bear a more plesanter vain, I wil leave the other to speake of them. *Tully*[Pg 33] defines them thus. *Comedia* (sayth he) is *Imitatio vitæ, speculum consuetudinis, et imago veritatis*, and it is sayde to be termed of *Comai* (emongste the Greekes) whiche signifieth *Pagos*, and *Ode, Cantus*: for that they were exercised in the fielde. They had they beginning wyth tragedies, but their matter was more plessaunt, for they were suche as did reprehend, yet *quodam lepore*. These first very rudely were invented by *Susarion Bullus*, and *Magnes* t[w]o aunctient poets, yet so that they were mervelous profitable to the reclamynge of abuse: whereupon *Eupolis* with *Cratinus*, and *Aristophanes* began to write, and with ther eloquenter vaine and perfection of stil[e], dyd more severely speak agaynst the abuses the[n] they: which *Horace* himselfe witnesseth. For sayth he ther was no abuse but these men reprehended it. A thefe was loth to be seene on there spectacle. A coward was never present at theyr assemblies. A backbiter abhord that company, and I my self could not have blamed your (Gosson) for exempting yourselfe from this theater, of troth I should have lykt your pollicy. These therefore, these wer they that kept men in awe, these restrayned the unbridled cominaltie, whereupon *Horace* wisely sayeth,

Oderunt peccare boni, virtutis amore,
Oderunt peccare mali, formidine penæ.

The good did hate al sinne for vertues love,
The bad for feare of shame did sin remove.

[Pg 34]

Yea would God our realme could light uppon a *Lucillius*, then should the wicked bee poynted out from the good, a harlot woulde seeke no harbor at stage plais, lest she shold here her owne name growe in question: and the discourse of her honesty cause her to bee hated of the godly. As for you I am sure of this one thing, he would paint you in your players orname[n]ts, for they best becam you. But as these sharpe corrections were disanulde in Rome when they grewe to more licenciousnes: so I fear me if we shold practise it in our dayes, the same intertainmente would followe. But in illreformed Rome what comedies now? A poets wit can correct, yet not offend. *Philemon* will mitigate the corrections of sinne, by reproving them covertly in shadowes. *Menandar* dare not offend ye Senate openly, yet wants he not a parasite to touch them prively. *Terence* wyl not report the abuse of harlots under there proper stile, but he can finely girde the[m] under the person of *Thais*. Hee dare not openly tell the Rich of theyr covetousnesse and severity towards their children, but he can controle them under the person of *Durus Demeas*. He must not shew the abuse of noble yong gentilmen under theyr owne title, but he wyll warne them in the person of *Pamphilus*. Wil you learne to know a parasite? Looke upon his *Dauus*. Wyl you seke the abuse of courtly flatterers? Behold *Gnato*: and if we had some Satericall Poetes nowe a[Pg 35] dayes to penn our commedies, that might be admitted of zeale to discypher the abuses of the worlde in the person of notorious offenders. I know we should wisely ryd our assemblyes of many of your brotherhod, but because you may have a full scope to reprehende, I will ryp up a rableme[n]t of playmakers, whose wrightinges I would wishe you overlooke, and seeke out theyr abuses. Can you mislike of *Cecillius*? or dispise

Plinius? or amend *Neuius*? or find fault with *Licinius*? Wherein offended *Actilius*? I am sure you can not but wonder at *Terrence*? Wil it please you to like of *Turpelius*? or alow of *Trabea*? You muste needs make much of *Ennius* for overloke al thes, and you shal find ther volums ful of wit if you examine the[m]: so yt if you had no other masters, you might deserve to be a doctor, wher now you are but a folishe scholemaister. But I wyll deale wyth you verye freendlye, I wil resolve everi doubt that you find. Those instrumentes which you mislike in playes grow of auncient custome, for when *Rossius* was an Actor, be sure that as with his tears he moved affections, so the Musitian in the Theater before the entrance, did mornefully record it in melody (as Servius reporteth). The actors in Rome had also gay clothing and every ma[n]s aparel was apliable to his part and person. The old men in white, ye rich men in purple, the parasite disguisedly, the yong men in gorgeous coulours, ther wanted no devise nor good[Pg 36] judgeme[n]t of ye comedy, whe[n]c[e] I suppose our players both drew ther plaies and fourme of garments. As for the appointed dayes wherin comedies wer showen, I reede that the Romaynes appoynted them on the festival dayes, in such reputation were they had at that time. Also *Iodocus Badius* will assertain you that the actors for shewing pleasure receved some profite. But let me apply those dayes to ours, their actors to our players, their autors to ours.

Surely we want not a *Rossius*, nether ar ther great scarsity of *Terrences* professio[n], but yet our men dare not nowe a dayes presume so much as the old Poets might, and therfore they apply ther writing to the peoples vain, wheras if in the beginning they had ruled, we should now adaies have found smal spectacles of folly. But (of truth) I must confes with *Aristotle*, that men are greatly delighted with imitation, and that it were good to bring those things on stage, that were altogether tending to vertue: all this I admit, and hartely wysh, but you say unlesse the thinge be taken away the vice will continue, nay I say if the style were changed the practise would profit. And sure I thinke our theaters fit, that *Ennius* seeing our wa[n]ton *Glicerium* may rebuke her, if our poetes will nowe become severe, and for prophane things write of vertue: you I hope shoulde see a reformed state in those thinges, which I feare me yf they were not, the idle hedded commones would worke more mis[Pg 37]chiefe. I wish as zealously as the best that all abuse of playinge were abolished, but for the thing, the antiquitie causeth me to allow it, so it be used as it should be. I cannot allow the prophaning of the Sabaoth, I praise your reprehension in that, you did well in discommending the abuse, and surely I wysh that that folly wer disclaymed, it is not to be admitted, it maks those sinne, which perhaps if it were not, would have binne present at a good sermon. It is in the Magistrate to take away that order, and appoynt it otherwyse. But sure it were pittie to abolish yt which hath so great vertue in it, because it is abused. The Germanes when the use of preaching was forbidden them, what helpe had they I pray you? Forsoth the learned were fayne covertly in comodies to declare abuses, and by playing to incite the people to vertues, whe[n] they might heare no preaching. Those were lamentable dayes you will say, and so thinke I, but was not this I pray you a good help in reforming the decaying Gospel? You see then how comedies (my severe judges) are requesit both for ther antiquity, and for ther commoditye: for the dignity of the wrighters, and the pleasure of the hearers. But after your discrediting of playmaking, you salve uppon the sore somewhat, and among many wise workes there be some that fitte your vaine: the practise of parasites is one, which I mervel it likes you so well since it bites you so sore. But sure in that I like[Pg 38] your judgement, and for the rest to[o], I approve your wit, but for the pigg of your own sow (as you terme it) assuredly I must discommend your verdit. Tell me Gosson was all your owne you wrote there: did you borow nothing of your neyghbours? but of what booke patched you out *Ciceros* oration? Whence fet you *Catulins* invective? Thys is one thing, *alienam olet lucernâ non tuam*. So that your helper may wisely reply upon you with *Virgil*,

Hos ego versiculos feci tulit alter honores,

I made these verses other bear the name. Beleve me I should preferr Wilsons, shorte and sweete if I were judge, a peece surely worthy prayse, the practise of a good scholler, would the wiser would overlooke that, they may perhaps cull some wisedome out of a players toye. Well, as it is wisedome to commend where the cause requireth, so it is a poynt of folly to praise without deserte. You dislike players very much, theyr dealings be not for your commodity, whom if I myghte advise they should learne thys of *Juvenal*:

Vivendum est recte
Cum propter plurima, tum his
Præcipue causis: ut linguas mancipiorum
Contēnas. Nā lingua mali pars pessima servi.

We ought to leade our lives aright,
For many causes move.
Especially for this same cause,
Wisedome doth us behove.
[Pg 39]

That we may set at nough[t] those blames,
Which servants to us lay,
For why, the tongue of evel slave,
Is worst as wise men ever say.

Methinks I heare some of them verifiing these verses upon you, if it so be that I hear them, I wil concele it, as for the statute of apparrell and the abuses thereof, I see it manifestly broken, and if I should seeke for example, you cannot but offend my eyes. For if you examine the statuts exactly, a simple cote should be fitted to your backe. We should bereve you of your braverye, and examine your au[n]cestry, and by profession in respect of ye statute, we should find you catercosens with a (but hush), you know my meaning, I must for pitie favor your credit in that you weare once a scholler. You runne farther to Carders, dicers, fencers, bowlers, dauncers, and tomblers, whose abuses I wold rebuke with you, had not your self moved other matters. But to eche I say thus, for dicing I wyshe those that know it not to leave to learn it, and let the fall of others make them wiser. Yf they had an *Alexander* to govern they shold be punished, and I could wish them not to abuse the lenitie of their prince. *Cicero* for a great blemish reputeth that which our gentilmen use for bravery, but *sufficit ista leniter attigisse*, a word against fencers, and so an end. Whom I wish to beware with *Demonax* lest[Pg 40] admitting theyr fencing delightes, they destroy (with the *Athenians*) the alters of peace; by raysing quarrellous causes, they worke uprores: but you and I reprove the[m] in abuse, yet I (for my part) cannot but allow the practise so it be well used. As for the filling of our gracious princes cofers with peace, as it pertaineth not to me, because I am none of her receivors, so men think unlesse it hath bine lately you have not bene of her majesties counsel. But now here as you begin folishly, so surely you end unlernedly. Prefer you warre before peace? the sword before the Goune? the rule of a Tyrant before ye happy days of our gracious Queen? You know the philosophers are against you, yet dare you stand in handy grips wyth *Cicero*: you know that force is but an instrume[n]t when counsell fayleth, and if wisedome win not, farwel warre. Aske *Alphonsus* what counsellors he lyketh of? hee will say his bookes: and hath not I pray you pollicy alwais over-mastered force? Who subdued *Hannibal* in his great royalty? he yt durst knock at Rome gates to have the[m] opened is nowe become a pray to a sylly senator. *Appius Claudius et senex et cæcus*, a father full of wisedome can releve the state of decaying Rome. And was it force that subdued *Marius*? or armes that discovered *Catulins* conspiracies? Was it rash reuendg in punishing *Cethegus*? or want of witt in the discoverye of treason? *Cato* can correct him[Pg 41]selfe for traveling by Sea, when the land profereth passage, or to be fole hardy in over mutch hazard. *Aristotle* accompteth counsell holye, and *Socrates* can terme it the key of certentye. What shall we count of war but wrath, of battel but hastines, and if I did rule (with *Augustus Cæsar*) I woulde refuse these counselers. What made ye oracle I praye you accompt of *Calchas* so much? was it not for his wisedome? who doth not like of the governer that had rather meete with *Unum Nestorem* than *decem Aiaces*? You cannot tame a Lyon but in tyme, neither a Tigres in few dayes. Counsell in *Regulus* will preferring the liberty of his country before his lyfe, not remit the delivery of *Carthaginian* captives. *Hannibal* shall flesh himselfe on an olde mans carkas, whose wisedom preserved his citye. *Adrian* with letters can governe hys legions, and rule peasablye his provinces by policye. Aske *Silvius Italicus* what peace is and he will say:

Pax optima rerum quas homini novisse
datum est, pax una triumphis
Innumeris potior, pax custodire salutem.
Et cives æquare potens.

No better thing to man did nature
Ever give then peace,
Then which to know no greater joy
Can come to our encrease.
To foster peace is stay of health,
And keepes the land in ease.

[Pg 42]

Take cou[n]sell of Ovid what sayth he?

Candida pax homines, trux decet atra feras.

To men doth heavenly peace pertaine
And currish anger fitteth brutish vaine.

Well as I wish it to have continuance, so I praye God wyth the Prophet it be not abused. And because I think my selfe to have sufficiently answered that I supposed, I conclude with this. God preserve our peacable princes[s], and confound her enemies. God enlarge her wisdome, that like *Saba* she may seeke after a *Salomon*: God confounde the imaginations of her enemies, and perfit His graces in her, that the daies of her rule may be continued in the bonds of peace, that the house of the chosen Isralites may be maynteyned in happinesse: lastly I frendly bid Gosson farwell, wyshinge him to temper his penn with more discretion.

[Pg 43]

II.—JOHN LYLY (?)

(*The author of* Euphues *is the most probable claimant for the authorship also of the following, which is perhaps the ablest and not the least characteristic of all the set, Martinist or anti-Martinist. The introduction and the notes will supply all absolutely necessary information for understanding it.*)

Pappe with an hatchet.

Alias,

A figge for my God sonne.

Or

Cracke me this nut.

Or

A Countrie cuffe, that is, a sound boxe of the eare, for the idiot Martin *to hold his peace, seeing the patch will take no warning.*

Written by one that dares call a dog, a dog, and made to preuent Martins *dog daies.*

Imprinted by *Iohn Anoke*, and *Iohn Astile*, for the Bayliue of Withernam, *cum priuilegio perennitatis*, and are to bee sold at the signe of the crab tree cudgell in thwackcoate lane.

A sentence.

Martin hangs fit for my mowing.

To the Father and the two Sonnes,
Huffe, Ruffe, and Snuffe,
the three tame ruffians of the Church, which take pepper
in the nose, because they can not
marre Prelates:
grating.

Roome for a royster; so thats well sayd, itch a little further for a good fellowe. Now haue at you all my gaffers of the rayling religion, tis I that must take you a peg lower. I am sure you looke for more worke, you shall haue wood enough to cleaue, make your tongue the wedge, and your head the beetle, Ile make such a splinter runne into your wits, as shal make thē ranckle till you become fooles. Nay, if you shoot bookes like fooles bolts, Ile be so bold as to make your iudgements quiuer with my thunderbolts. If you meane to gather clowdes in the Commonwealth, to threaten tempests, for your flakes of snowe weele pay you with stones of hayle; if with an Easterlie winde you bring Catterpillers into the Church, with a Northerne wind weele driue barrennes into your wits.

We care not for a Scottish mist, though it wet vs to the skin, you shal be sure your cockscombs shall not be mist, but pearst to the skuls. I professe rayling, and think it as good a cudgell for a Martin, as a stone for a dogge, or a whippe for an Ape, or poyson for a rat.

Yet find fault with no broad termes, for I haue mesured yours with mine, and I find yours broader iust by the list. Say not my speaches are light, for I haue weighed yours and mine, and I finde yours lighter by twentie graines than the allowance. For number you exceede, for you haue thirtie ribauld words for my one, and yet you beare a good spirit. I was loath so to write as I haue done, but that I learnde, that he that drinkes with cutters, must not be without his ale dagger; nor hee that buckles with Martin, without his lauish termes.

Who would currie an Asse with an Iuorie combe? giue the beast thistles for prouender. I doo but yet angle with a silken flye, to see whether Martins will nibble; and if I see that, why then I haue wormes for the nonce, and will giue them line enough like a[Pg 47] trowte, till they swallow both hooke and line, and then Martin beware your gilles, for Ile make you daunce at the poles end.

I knowe Martin will with a trice bestride my shoulders. Well, if he ride me, let the foole sit fast, for my wit is verie kickish; which if he spurre with his copper replie, when it bleedes, it will all to besmeare their consciences.

If a Martin can play at chestes, as well as his nephewe the ape, he shall knowe what it is for a scaddle pawne to crosse a Bishop in his owne walke. Such dydoppers must be taken vp, els theile not stick to check the king. Rip vp my life, discipher my name, fill thy answer as full of lies as of lines, swell like a toade, hisse like an adder, bite like a dog, and chatter like a monkey, my pen is prepared and my minde; and if yee chaunce to finde any worse words than you brought, let them be put in your dads dictionarie. And so farewell, and be hangd, and I pray God ye fare no worse.

                     Yours at an houres warning
                           Double V.

[Pg 48]

TO THE INDIFFERENT READER.

It is high time to search in what corner of the Church the fire is kindled, being crept so far, as that with the verie smoke the consciences of diuers are smothered. It is found that certaine Martins, if no miscreants in religion (which wee may suspect) yet without doubt malecōtents (which wee ought to feare) haue throwen fire, not into the Church porch, but into the Chauncell, and though not able by learning and iudgement to displace a Sexton, yet seeke to remooue Bishops. They haue scattered diuers libels, all so taunting and slanderous, as it is hard to iudge, whether their lyes exceed their bitternesse, or their bitternesse their fables.

If they be answered by the grauitie of learned Prelates, they presentlie reply with railings; which argueth their intent to be as farre frō the truth of deuotion, as their writings from mildnes of spirit. It is said that camels neuer drinke, till they haue troubled the water with their feete, and it seemes these Martins cannot carouse the sapp of the Church, till by faction they make tumults in religion. Seeing thē either they expect no graue replie, or that they are settled with railing to replie; I thought it more conuenient, to giue them a whisk with their owne wand, than to haue them spurd with deeper learning.

The Scithian slaues, though they bee vp in armes, must bee tamde with whippes, not swords, and these mutiners in Church matters, must haue their mouthes bungd with iests, not arguments.

I seldome vse to write, and yet neuer writ anie thing, that in speech might seeme vndecent, or in sense vnhonest; if here I haue vsed bad tearmes, it is because they are not to bee answered with good tearmes: for whatsoeuer shall seeme lauish in this Pamphlet, let it be thought borrowed of Martins language. These Martins were hatcht of addle egges, els could they not haue such idle heads. They measure conscience by their owne yard, and like the theeues, that had an yron bed, in which all that were too long they would cut euen, all that were too short they would stretch out, and none escapte vnrackt or vnsawed, that were not iust of their beds length: so all that are not Martins, that is, of their peeuish mind, must be measured by them. If he come short of their religion, why he is but a colde Protestant, hee must bee pluckt out to the length of a Puritane. If any be more deuout than they are, as to giue almes, fast, and pray, then they cut him off close by the workes, and say he is a Papist. If one be not cast in Martins mould, his religion must needes mould. He saith he is a Courtier, I thinke no[Pg 50] Courtier so peruerse, that seeing the streight rule of the Church, would goe about to bend it. It may be he is some Iester about the Court, and of that I meruaile, because I know all the fooles there, and yet cannot gesse at him. What euer he be, if his conscience be pind to his cognizance, I will account him more politicke than religious, and more dangerous for ciuill broyles, than the Spaniard for an open warre. I am ignorant of Martin and his maintainer, but my conscience is my warrant, to care for neither. For I knowe there is none of honour so carelesse, nor any in zeale so peeuish, nor of nature any so barbarous, that wil succour those that be suckers of the Church, a thing against God and policie; against God, in subuerting religion; against policie, in altering gouernment, making in the Church the feast of the Lapithees, where all shall bee throwne on anothers head, because euerie one would be the head. And these it is high time to tread vnder foote: for who would not make a threshold of those, that go about to make the Church a barne to thresh in. *Itaque sic disputo.*

FINIS.

[Pg 51]

PAPPE WITH AN HATCHET

Good morrow, goodman Martin, good morrow: will ye anie musique this morning? What, fast a sleepe? Nay faith, Ile cramp thee till I wake thee. *O whose tat?* Nay gesse olde knaue and odd knaue: for Ile neuer leaue pulling, till I haue thee out of thy bed into the streete; and then all shall see who thou art, and thou know what I am.

Your Knaueship brake you fast on the Bishops, by breaking your iests on them: but take heed you breake not your owne necke. Bastard Iunior dinde vpon them, and cramde his maw as full of mallice, as his head was of malapertnesse. Bastard Senior was with them at supper, and I thinke tooke a surfet of colde and raw quipps. O what queasie girds were they towards the fall of the leafe. Old Martin, neuer entaile thy wit to the eldest, for hee'le spend all he hath in a quire of paper.

> *Hee sweares by his mazer, that he will make their wits wetshod, if the ale haue his swift current.*

Now sirs, knowing your bellies full of Bishops bobbs, I am sure your bones would be at rest: but[Pg 52] wee'le set vp all our rests, to make you all restie. I was once determined to write a proper newe Ballet, entituled *Martin and his Maukin*, to no tune, because Martin was out of all tune. Elderton swore hee had rimes lying a steepe in ale, which should marre all your reasons: there is an olde hacker that shall take order for to print them. O how hee'le cut it, when his ballets come out of the lungs of the licour. They shall be better than those of Bonner, or the ierkes for a Iesuit. The first begins, Come tit me come tat me, come throw a halter at me.

Then I thought to touch Martin with Logick, but there was a little wag in Cambridge, that swore by Saint Seaton, he would so swinge him with Sillogismes, that all Martins answeres should ake. The vile boy hath manie bobbes, and a whole fardle of fallacies. He begins,

Linquo coax ranis, cros coruis, vanaque vanis.
Ad Logicam pergo, quæ Mart'ins non timet ergo.

And saies, he will ergo Martin into an ague. I haue read but one of his arguments.

Tiburne stands in the cold,
But Martins are a warme furre;
Therefore Tiburne must be furd with Martins.

O (quoth I) boy thou wilt be shamed; tis neither[Pg 53] in moode nor figure: all the better, for I am in a moode to cast a figure, that shall bring them to the conclusion. I laught at the boye, and left him drawing all the lines of Martin into sillogismes, euerie conclusion beeing this, Ergo Martin is to bee hangd.

Nay, if rime and reason bee both forestalde, Ile raile, if Martin haue not barrelde vp all rakehell words: if he haue, what care I to knock him on the head with his owne hatchet. He hath taken vp all the words for his obscenitie: obscentie? Nay, now I am too nice; squirrilitie were a better word: well, let me alone to squirrell them.

Martin, thinkst thou, thou hast so good a wit, as none can outwrangle thee? Yes Martin, wee will play three a vies wits: art thou so backt that none dare blade it with thee? Yes Martin, wee will drop vie stabbes. Martin sweares I am some gamester. Why, is not gaming lawful? I know where there is more play in the compasse of an Hospitall, than in the circuite of Westchester. One hath been an old stabber at passage: the One that I meane, thrust a knife into ones thigh at Cambridge, the quarrel was about cater-tray, and euer since he hath quarrelled about cater-caps.

I thought that hee which thrust at the bodie in game, would one daie cast a foyne at the soule in earnest. But hee workes closelie and sees all, hee[Pg 54] learnd that of old Vydgin the cobler, who wrought ten yeares with spectacles, and yet swore he could see through a dicker of leather. He hath a wanton spleene, but wee will haue it stroakt with a spurne, because his eies are bleard, he thinkes to bleare all ours; but let him take this for a warning, or else looke for such a warming, as shall make all his deuices as like wood, as his spittle is like woodsere. Take away the Sacke, and giue him some Cinamom water, his conscience hath a colde stomacke. Cold? Thou art deceiued, twil digest a Cathedral Church as easilie as an Estritch a two penie naile.

But softe Martins, did your Father die at the Groyne? It was well groapt at, for I knewe him sicke of a paine in the groyne. A pockes of that religion (quoth Iulian Grimes to her Father) when al his haires fell off on the sodaine. Well let the olde knaue be dead. Whie are not the spawnes of such a dog-fish hangd? Hang a spawne? drowne it; alls one, damne it.

Ye like not a Bishops rochet, when all your fathers hankerchers were made of his sweete harts smocke. That made you bastards, and your dad a cuckold, whose head is swolne so big, that he had neede sende to the cooper to make him a biggin: and now you talke of a cooper, Ile tell you a tale of a tubb.

> They are not so many, thei are all Centimani, an hundred hands a peece: so that in all they are but one thousand.

At Sudburie, where the Martin-mōgers swarmd to a lecture, like beares to a honnie pot: a good honest[Pg 55] strippling, of the age of fiftie yeares or thereabout, that could haue done a worse act if companie had not been neere, askt his sweete sister, whether lecherie in her conscience were a sinne? In faith (quoth she) I thinke it the superficies of sinne, and no harme if the tearmes be not abusde, for you must say, vertuously done, not lustily done. Fie, this is filthie ribaldry. O sir, ther is no mirth without ribaldrie, nor ribaldrie without Martin, ask mine hostesse of the iuie bush in Wye for the one, and my old hostesse of the Swanne in Warwicke for the other. She is dead: the diuell she is. You are too broad with Martins brood: for hee hath a hundred thousand that will set their handes to his Articles, and shewe the Queene. Sweeter and sweeter: for wee haue twentie hundred thousand handes to withstand them. I would it were come to the grasp, we would show them an Irish tricke, that when they thinke to winne the game with one man, wee'le make holde out till wee haue but two left to carrie them to the gallowes: well followed in faith, for thou saidst thou wert a gamester. All this is but bad English, when wilt thou come to a stile? Martin hath manie good words. Manie? Now you put me in minde of the matter, there is a booke cōming out of a hundred merrie tales, and the petigree of Martin, fetchte from the burning of Sodome, his [Pg 56] armes shal be set on his hearse, for we are prouiding his funerall, and for the winter nights the tales shall be told *secundum vsum Sarum*: the Deane of Salisburie can tell twentie. If this will not make Martin mad, malicious and melancholie (ô braue letter followed with a full crie) then will we be desperate, and hire one that shall so translate you out of French into English, that you will blush and lie by it. And one will we coniure vp, that writing a familiar Epistle about the naturall causes of an Earthquake, fell into the bowells of libelling, which made his eares quake for feare of clipping, he shall tickle you with taunts; all his works bound close, are at least six sheetes in quarto, and he calls them the first tome of his familiar Epistle: he is full of latin endes, and worth tenne of those that crie in London, *haie ye anie gold ends to sell*. If he giue you a bob, though he drawe no bloud, yet are you sure of a rap with a bable. If he ioyne with vs, *perijsti* Martin, thy wit wil be massacred: if the toy take him to close with thee, then haue I my wish, for this tenne yeres haue I lookt to lambacke him. Nay he is a mad lad, and such a one as cares as little for writing without wit, as Martin doth for writing without honestie; a notable coach companion for Martin, to drawe Diuinitie from the Colledges of Oxford and Cambridge, to Shoomakers hall in Sainct Martins. But we neither feare Martin, nor the foot-cloth, nor the beast that wears [Pg 57] it, be he horse or asse; nor whose sonne he is, be he Martins sonne, Iohns sonne, or Richards sonne; nor of what occupation he be, be a ship-wright, cart-wright, or tiburn-wright. If they bring seuen hundred men, they shall be boxt with fourteen hundred boyes. Nay we are growing to a secret bargaine. O, but I forgate a riddle; *the more it is spied, the lesse it is seene*. Thats the Sunne: the lesse it is spied of vs, the more it is seene of those vnder vs. The Sunne? thou art an asse, it is the Father, for the old knaue, thinking by his bastardie to couer his owne heade, putteth it like a stagge ouer the pale. Pale? nay I will make him blush as red as ones nose, that was alwaies washt in well water.

What newes from the Heraldes? Tush, thats time enough to know to morrow, for the sermon is not yet cast. The sermon foole? why they neuer studie, but cleaue to Christ his *dabitur in illa hora*. They venter to catch soules, as they were soles; Doctors are but dunces, none sowes true stitches in a pulpet, but a shoomaker.

> Martin Iunior saies, hee found his fathers papers vnder a bush, the knaue was started from his Fourme.

Faith, thou wilt bee caught by the stile. What care I to be found by a stile, when so many Martins haue been taken vnder an hedge? If they cannot leuell, they will roue at thee, and anatomize thy life from the cradle to the graue, and thy bodie from the corne on thy toe, to the crochet on thy [Pg 58] head. They bee as cunning in cutting vp an honest mans credit, as Bull in quartering a knaues bodie. Tush (what care I) is my posie; if hee meddle with mee, Ile make his braines so hot that they shall crumble, and rattle in his warpt scull, like pepper in a dride bladder.

I haue a catalogue of al the sheepe, and it shall go hard, but I will crosse the bel-weather. Why shuld I feare him that walkes on his neats-feete. Neither court, nor countrie that shal be free, I am like death, Ile spare none. There shall not misse a name of anie, that had a Godfather; if anie bee vnchristened, Ile nicke him with a name.

But whist; beware an action of the case. Then put this for the case, whether it bee not as lawfull to set downe the facts of knaues, as for a knaue to slander honest men. Alls as it is taken; marie the diuell take al, if truth find not as many soft cushions to leane on as trecherie.

Theres one with a lame wit, which will not weare a foure cornerd cap, then let him put on Tiburne, that hath but three corners; and yet the knaue himselfe hath a pretie wench in euerie corner.

> *He calls none but the heavens to witnesse.*

I could tickle Martin with a true tale of one of his sonnes, that hauing the companie of one of his sisters in the open fieldes, saide, hee would not smoother vp sinne, and deale in hugger mugger against his Conscience. In the hundred[Pg 59] merrie tales, the places, the times, the witnesses and all, shall be put downe to the proofe, where I warrant you, the Martinists haue consciences of proofe. Doost think Martin, thou canst not be discouered? What foole would not thinke him discouered that is balde? Put on your night cap, and your holie day English, and the best wit you haue for high daies, all wil be little enough to keep you from a knaues penance, though as yet you bee in a fooles paradice. If you coyen words, as *Cankerburie*, *Canterburines*, etc. whie, I know a foole that shall so inkhornize you with straunge phrases, that you shall blush at your owne bodges. For Similes, theres another shal liken thee to anie thing, besides he can raile too. If Martin muzzle not his mouth, and manacle his hands, Ile blabb all, and not sticke to tell, that pewes and stewes are rime in their religion.

Scratch not thy head Martin, for be thou Martin the bird, or Martin the beast; a bird with the longest bill, or a beast with the longest eares, theres a net spread for your necke. Martin, Ile tell thee a tale woorth twelue pence, if thy witt bee woorth a pennie.

There came to a Duke in Italie, a large lubber and a beggerlie, saying hee had the Philosophers Stone, and that hee could make golde faster than the Duke could spend it. The Duke askt him why hee made none to mainteine himself? Because, quoth he, I could neuer get a secret place to worke[Pg 60] in; for once I endeuoured, and the Popes holinesse sent for me, whom if he had caught, I should haue been a prentice to mainteine his pride. The Duke minding to make triall of his cunning, and eager of golde, set him to worke closely in a vault, where it was not knowen to his neerest seruants. This Alcumist, in short time consumed two thousande pound of the Dukes gold, and brought him halfe a ducket: whie (quoth the Duke) is this all? All, quoth he, my Lord, that I could make by Art. Wel said the Duke then shalt thou see my cunning: for I will boile thee, straine thee, and then drie thee, so that of a lubber, that weighed three hundred weight, I will at last make a dram of knaues powder. The Duke did it.

> Martin and his mainteiner are both sawers of timber, but Martin stands in the pit, all the dust must fall in his eies, but he shal neuer walke on the boards.

Martin, if thou to cousen haue crept into the bosome of some great mē, saying thou hast the churches discipline, and that thou canst by thy faction and pollicie pull down Bishops and set vp Elders, bring the lands of the Clergy into the cofers of the Temporaltie, and repaire Religion, by impairing their liuings, it may bee, thou shalt bee hearkened too, stroakt on the head, greasd in the hand, fed daintelie, kept secretlie, and countenaunst mightelie. But when they perceiue that all thy deuices bee but Chymeraes, monsters of thine owne imaginations, so farre from pulling downe a Cathedrall Church, that they cannot remooue a corner of a square[Pg 61] cap, thē will they deale with thee as the Duke did with the Alcumist, giue thee as many bobs on the eare as thou hast eaten morsels of their meate, and make thee an example of sedition to be pointed at, that art now so mewde vp that none can point where thou art. All this tale, with the application, was not of my penning, but found among loose papers; marie he that did it, dares stand to it. Now, because I haue nothing to doo betweene this and supper, Ile tell you another tale, and so begin Winter by time.

There was a libeller, who was also a coniurer, so that whatsoeuer casting of figures there was, he deceiued them; at the last, one as cunning as himself, shewed, wher he sate writing in a fooles coate, and so he was caught and whipt. Martin, there are figures a flinging, and ten to one thou wilt be found sitting in a Knaues skinne, and so be hangd.

Hollow there, giue me the beard I wore yesterday. O beware of a gray beard, and a balde head: for if such a one doo but nod, it is right dudgin and deepe discretion. But soft, I must now make a graue speach.

There is small difference between Swallowes and Martins, either in shape or nature, saue onely, that the Martins haue a more beetle head, they both breed in Churches, and hauing fledgde their young ones,[Pg 62] leaue nothing behind them but durt. Vnworthie to come into the Church porch, or to be nourished vnder anie good mans eues, that gnawe the bowels, in which they were bred, and defile the place, in which they were ingendred.

They studie to pull downe Bishopps, and set vp Superintendents, which is nothing else but to raze out good Greeke, and enterline bad Latin. A fine period; but I cannot continue this stile, let me fal into my olde vaine. O doost remember, howe that Bastard Iunior complaines of brothells, and talkes of long Megg of Westminster. A craftie iacke, you thoght because you twitted Mar-martin, that none would suspect you; yes faith Martin, you shall bee thresht with your owne flaile.

> *Hee thought Lais had still lien at Corinth as wel as Paul.*

It was one of your neast, that writt this for a loue letter, to as honest a womā as euer burnt malt. 'Grace, mercie, and peace to thee (O widow) with feruent motions of the spirit, that it may worke in thee both to will and to doo. Thou knowest my loue to thee is, as Paules was to the Corinthians; that is, the loue of copulation.'

How now holie Martin, is this good wooing? If you prophane the Scriptures, it is a pretie wit; if we but alledge Doctors to expound them, wee are wicked. If Martin oppresse his neighbor, why, hee saith, it is his conscience; if anie else doo right, it is extremitie. Martin may better goe into a brothell house, then anie other go by it; he slides into a bad place like the Sunne, all others stick in it like pitch. If Martin speake broad bawdrie, why all the crue saies, your worship is passing merrie. Martin will not sweare, but with indeede, in sooth, and in truth, hee'le cogge the die of deceipt, and cutte at the bumme carde of his conscience. O sweetelie brought in, at least three figures in that line, besides the wit ant.

One there was, and such a one as Martin would make the eldest of his Elders, that hauing fortie angels sent him for a beneuolence, refusde to giue the poore fellowe a quittance for the receipt, saying, Christ had giuen his master a quittance, the same howre he told it out: and this was at his table, where he sate with no less than fortie good dishes of the greatest dainties, in more pompe than a Pope, right like a superintendent.

Now to the two bastards, what, were you twins? It shuld seeme so, for ther wēt but a paire of sheeres betweene your knaueries. When the old henne hatcht such eggs, the diuell was in the cocks comb. Your father thrusts you forward, remember pettie Martins Aesops crab, the mother going backward, exhorted her sonnes to goe forward; doo you so first mother, quoth they, and we will follow. Now the old cuckold hath puld in his hornes, he would make you creepe cleane out of the shell, and so both loose your houses and shewe your nakednesse. You go about impossibilities, wele no such chāge, and if ye had it, ye would be wearie of it.

There was a man like Martin that had a goose, which euerie daie laid him a golden egge, he, not content with the blessing, kild his goose, thinking to haue a myne of golde in her bellie, and finding nothing but dung, the gāder wisht his goose aliue. Martinists that liue well by the Church, and receiue great benefites of it, thinke if all

Churches were downe they should be much better, but when they shall see cōfusion instead of discipline, and atheisme to be found in place of doctrine, will they not with sighs wish the Churches and Bishops in their wonted gouernmēt? Thou art well seen in tales, and preachest Aesops fables. Tush, Ile bring in *Pueriles*, and *Stans puer ad mensam*, for such vnmannerlie knaues as Martin must bee set againe to their A.B.C. and learn to spell Our Father in a Horne books. Martin Iunior giues warning that none write against reuerent Martin: yes, there are *a tribus ad centum*, from three to an hūdred, that haue vowed to write him out of his right wittes, and we are all *Aptots*, in all cases alike, till we haue brought Martin to the ablatiue case, that is, to bee taken away with Bulls voyder.

O here were a notable full point, to leaue Martin in the hangmans apron. Nay, he would be glad to scape with hanging, weele first haue him lashte[Pg 65] through the Realme with cordes, that when hee comes to the gallowes he may be bleeding new.

The babie comes in with *Nunka*, *Næme*, and *Dad* (Pappe with an hatchet for such a puppie), giue the infant a bibbe, he all to beslauers his mother tongue, if he driuell so at the mouth and nose, weele haue him wipte with a hempen wispe. *Hui?* How often hast thou talkt of haltring? Whie it runnes still in my minde that they must be hangd. Hangde is the Que, and it comes iust to my purpose.

There was one endited at a Iaile deliuerie of felonie, for taking vp an halter by the high way. The Iurie gaue verdit and said guiltie. The Iudge an honest man, said it was hard to find one guiltie for taking vp a penie halter, and bad them consider, what it was to cast awaie a man. Quoth the foreman, we haue enquired throughly, and found there was a horse tied to the halter. I, marie (quoth the Iudge), then let him be tied to the halter, and let the horse goe home. Martin, a Monarch in his owne moyst conceit, and drie counsell, saies he is enuied onelie because he leuelleth at Bishops; and we say as the Iudge saith, that if there were nothing else it were hard to persecute them to death; but when we finde that to the rule of the Church, the whole state of the Realme is linckt, and that they filching away Bishop by Bishop, seeke to fish for the Crown, and glew to their newe Church their owne conclusions,[Pg 66] we must then say, let Bishops stand, and they hang; that is, goe home. Looke howe manie tales are in this booke, so manie must you abate of an hundred in the next booke, reckon this for one.

There came by of late a good honest Minister, with a cloake hauing sleeues: ah (quoth a Martinist, sitting on a bulke in Cheapside) he is a knaue I warrant you, a claspe would become one of his coate to claspe his cloak vnder his chinne. Where tis to be noted, that they come in with a sleeueless conscience, and thinke it no good doctrine which is not preached with the cloak cast ouer each shoulder like a rippier.

Twas a mad knaue and a Martinist that diuided his sermon into 34 parts for memorie sake, and would handle but foure for memorie sake, and they were, why Christ came, wherefore Christ came, for what cause Christ came, and to what end Christ came; this was all for memorie sake. If that Martin could thatch vp his Church, this mans scabship should bee an Elder, and Elders they may bee, which being fullest of spungie pith, proue euer the driest kixes. For in time you shall see that it is but a bladder of worldlie winde which swells in their hearts, being once prickt, the humour will quicklie be remoued, O what a braue state of the Church it would be for all Ecclesiasticall causes to come before Weauers and Wierdawers, to see one in a motlie Ierkin and an[Pg 67] apron to reade the first lesson. The poore Church should play at vnequal game, for it should loose al by the *Elder* hand. Nay Mas Martin, weele make you deale, shuffle as well as you can, we meane to cut it.

If you had the foddring of the sheep you would make the Church like Primero, foure religions in it, and nere one like another. I cannot out of his gaming humour. Why? Is it not as good as Martins dogged humour, who without reuerence, regard, or exception, vseth such vnfitting tearmes, as were hee the greatest subiect in England hee could not iustifie them.

Shut the doores (sirs) or giue me my skimmer, Martins mouth had sod vnskimde these twelue months, and now it runnes ouer; yet let him alone, he makes but porredge for the diuell.

His Elderberines though it be naught worth, yet is it like an elderberrie, which being at the ripenes of a perfect black, yet brused staines ones hands like bloud. They pretending grauitie in the rottennes of their zeale, bee they once wrung, you shall finde them lighter than feathers. Thats a simile for the slaues. Nay, Ile touch them deeper, and make them crie, O my heart, there is a false knaue among vs.

Take away this beard, and giue me a pickede vaunt, Martin sweares by his ten bones: nay, I will make him mumpe, mow, and chatter, like old Iohn of Paris garden before I leaue him.

[Pg 68]

If Martin will fight Citie fight, wee challenge him at all weapons, from the taylors bodkin to the watchmans browne bil. If a field may be pitcht we are readie: if they scratch, wee will bring cattes: if scolde, we will bring women: if multiplie words, we will bring fooles: if they floute, we will bring quippes: if dispute the matter, we will bring schollers: if they buffet, we will bring fists. *Deus bone*, what a number of we will brings be here? Nay, we will bring Bull to hang them. A good note and signe of good lucke, three times motion of Bull. Motion of Bull? Why, next olde Rosses motion of Bridewell, Buls motion fits them best. *Tria sequuntur tria*, in reckoning Bull thrise, methinkes it should presage hanging. O bad application; Bad? I doo not thinke there can be a better, than to applie a knaues necke to an halter. Martin cannot start, I am his shadowe, one parte of the day before him, another behinde him; I can chalke a knaue on his backe thrice a weeke, Ile let him bloud in the combe.

Take heed, he will pistle thee. Pistle me? Then haue I a pestle so to stampe his pistles, that Ile beate all his wit to powder. What will the powder of Martins wit be good for? Marie, blowe vp a dram of it into the nostrels of a good Protestant, it will make him giddie; but if you minister it like Tobacco to a Puritane, it will make him as mad as a Martin.

Goe to, a hatch before the doore, Martin smels[Pg 69] thee, and wil not feare thee; thou knowest how he deales with the Archbishop and a Counseller, hee will name thee and that broadlie. Name me? Mary he and his shall bee namefied, that's it I thirst after, that name to name, and knowing one another, wee may in the streetes grapple; wee except none: wee come with a verse in our mouthes, courage in our hearts, and weapons in our hands, and crie

Discite iustitiam moniti, et non temnere diuos.

Martins conscience hath a periwig; therefore to good men he is more sower than wig: a Lemman will make his conscience curd like a Posset. Now comes a biting speach, let mee stroake my beard thrice like a Germain, before I speak a wise word.

Martin, wee are now following after thee with hue and crie, and are hard at thy heeles; if thou turne backe to blade it, wee doubt not but three honest men shall bee able to beate six theeues. Weele teach thee to commit sacriledge, and to robbe the Church of xxiiij. Bishops at a blowe. Doost thinke that wee are not men Martin, and haue great men to defend vs which write? Yes, although with thy seditious cloase, thou would'st perswade her Maiestie that most of the Gentlemen of account and men of honour, were by vs thought Puritanes. No, it is your poore Iohns, that with your painted consciences[Pg 70] haue coloured the religion of diuers, spreading through the veynes of the Commonwealth like poyson, the doggednes of your deuotions; which entring in like the smoothnes of oyle into the flesh, fretteth in time like quicksiluer into the bones.

When children play with their meate, tis a signe their bellies are full, and it must be taken from them; but if they tread it vnder their feete, they ought to be ierkt. The Gospell hath made vs wantons, wee dallie with Ceremonies, dispute of circumstances, not remembring that the Papists haue been making roddes for vs this thirtie yeares; wee shall bee swing'd by them, or worse by Martin, if Martins be worse. Neuer if it, for they bee worse with a witnesse, and let the dieull be witnesse. Wee are so nice, that the Cap is a beame in our Church, the booke of Common Praier a milstone, the *Pater noster* is not well pend by Christ. Well, either religion is but policie, or policie scarce religious.

If a Gentleman riding by the way with twentie men, a number of theeues should by deuise or force binde all his seruants; the good Iustice of Peace would thinke he should be robd. When Martinists, rancke robbers of the Church, shall binde the legges and armes of the Church, me thinkes the supreme head of the Church should looke pale.

They that pull downe the bells of a steeple, and say it is conscience, will blow vp the chauncell to[Pg 71] make it the quintessence of conscience. Bir Ladie, this is a good settled speech, a Diuine might haue seemed to haue said so much. O sir, I am nor al tales, and riddles, and rimes, and iestes, thats but my Liripoope, if Martin knock the bone he shall find marrow, and if he looke for none, we'le knock the bone on his pate, and bring him on his marie bones.

I haue yet but giuen them a fillip on the conceipt, Ile fell it to the ground hereafter. Nay, if they make their consciences stretch like chiuerell in the raine, Ile make them crumple like parchment in the fire.

I haue an excellent balme to cure anie that is bitten with *Martin mad-dog*.

I am worth twentie Pistle-penners; let them but chafe my penne, and it shal sweat out a whole realme of paper, or make thē odious to the whole Realme.

O but be not partial, giue them their due though they were diuels, so will I, and excuse them for taking anie money at interest.

There is a good Ladie that lent one of these Martinists fortie pounds, and when at the daie shee required her money, Martin began to storme, and said, he thought her not the child of God, for they must lend, looking for nothing againe, and so to acquite himselfe of the blot of vsurie he kepte the principall.

These Martins make the Scriptures a Scriueners shop to drawe conueyances, and the common pleas [Pg 72] of Westminster to take forfeitures. Theyle not sticke to outlaw a mans soule, and serue it presently with an execution of damnation, if one denie them to lie with his neighbours wife. If they bee drunke, they say, they haue Timothie his weake stomacke, which Saint Paule willeth to warme with wine.

They haue sifted the holie Bible, and left vs nothing as they say, but branne; they haue boulted it ouer againe and againe, and got themselues the fine meale; tis meale indeede, for with their wresting and shuffling holie Writ, they find all themselues good meales, and stand at liuerie, as it were, at other mens tables.

Sed heus tu, dic sodes, will they not bee discouraged for the common players? Would those Comedies might be allowed to be plaid that are pend, and then I am sure he would be decyphered, and so perhaps discouraged.

He shall not bee brought in as whilom he was, and yet verie well, with a cocks combe, an apes face, a wolfs bellie, cats clawes, etc. but in a cap'de cloake, and all the best apparell he ware the highest day in the yeare, thats neither on Christmas daie, Good fridaie, Easter daie, Ascension, nor Trinitie sundaie (for that were popish), but on some rainie weeke-daie, when the brothers and sisters had appointed a match for particular praiers, a thing as bad at the least as Auricular confession.

[Pg 73]

> If it be shewed at Paules, it will cost you foure pence: at the Theater two pence: at Sainct Thomas a Watrings nothing.

A stage plaier, though he bee but a cobler by occupation, yet his chance may bee to play the Kings part. Martin, of what calling so euer he be, can play nothing but the knaues part, *qui tantum constans in knauitate sua est*. Would it not bee a fine Tragedie, when *Mardocheus* shall play a Bishoppe in a Play, and Martin *Hamman*, and that he that seekes to pull downe those that are set in authoritie aboue him, should be hoysted vpon a tree aboue all other.

> Reade Martin Seniors Libell, and you shall perceiue that he is able to teach Gracchus to speake seditiouslie.

Though he play least in sight now, yet we hope to see him stride from Aldgate to Ludgate, and looke ouer all the Citie at London Bridge. Soft swift, he is no traytor. Yes, if it bee treason to encourage the Commons against the chiefe of the Clergie, to make a generall reuolt from the gouernment so wel established, so wisely maintained, and so long prospering.

Because they say, *Aue Cæsar*, therefore they meane nothing against Cæsar. There may bee hidden vnder their long gownes short daggers, and so in blearing Cæsars eyes, conspire Cæsars death. God saue the Queene; why it is the Que which they take from the mouthes of all traytors, who though they bee throughly conuinced, both by proofe and their owne confessions, yet at the last gaspe they crie, God saue the Queene. GOD[Pg 74] saue the Queene (say I) out of their hands, in whose hearts (long may the Queene thus gouerne) is not engrauen.

Her sacred Maiestie hath this thirtie yeares, with a setled and princelie temper swayed the Scepter of this Realme, with no lesse content of her subiects, than wonder of the world. GOD hath blessed her gouernment, more by miracle thā by counsaile, and yet by counsaile as much as can come from policie. Of a State taking such deepe roote, as to be fastened by the prouidence of God, the vertue of the Prince, the wisedome of Counsellers, the obedience of subiects, and the length of time; who would goe about to shake the lowest bough, that feeles in his conscience but the least blessing. Heere is a fit roome to squese them with an Apothegme.

There was an aged man that liued in a well ordered Common-wealth by the space of threescore yeares, and finding at the length that by the heate of some mens braines, and the warmnes of other mens bloud, that newe alterations were in hammering, and that it grewe to such an height, that all the desperate and discontented persons were readie to runne their heads against their head; comming into the midst of these mutiners, cried as loude as his yeares would allow; Springalls and vnripened youthes, whose wisedomes are yet in the blade, when this snowe shall be melted (laying his hand on his siluer haires)[Pg 75] then shal you find store of durt, and rather wish for the continuance of a long frost, than the comming of an vntimely thaw. Ile moralize this.

Ile warrant the good old man meant, that when the ancient gouernment of the state should be altered by faction, or newe lawes brought in that were deuised by nice heads, that there should followe a foule and slipperie managing; where if happelie most did not fall, yet all would bee tired. A settled raigne is not like glasse mettal, to be blowne in bignesse, lenght or fashion of euerie mans breath, and breaking to be melted againe, and so blowne afresh; but it is compared to the fastning of the Cedar, that knitteth it selfe with such wreaths into the earth that it cannot be remooued by any violent force of the aire.

Martin, I haue taken an inuentorie of al thy vnciuill and rakehell tearmes, and could sute them in no place but in Bedlam and Bridewell, so mad they are, and so bad they are, and yet all proceedes of the spirit. I thinke thou art possest with the spirites of Iacke Straw and the Black-smith, who, so they might rent in peeces the gouernment, they would drawe cuts for religion.

If all be conscience, let conscience bee the foundation of your building, not the glasse, shew effects of conscience, mildnesse in spirit, obedience to Magistrates, loue to thy brethren. Stitch charitie to thy faith, or rip faith from thy works.

[Pg 76]

If thou wilt deale soberlie without scoffes, thou shalt be answered grauely without iests, yea and of those, whom thou canst not controll for learning, nor accuse for ill life, nor shouldst contemne for authori[ti]e. But if like a restie Iade thou wilt take the bitt in thy mouth, and then runne ouer hedge and ditch, thou shalt be brokē as Prosper broke his horses, with a muzroule, portmouth, and a martingall, and so haue thy head runne against a stone wall.

If thou refuse learning, and sticke to libelling; if nothing come out of those lauish lips, but taunts not without bitternesse, yet without wit; rayling not without spite, yet without cause, then giue me thy hand, thou and I will trie it out at the cuckingstoole. Ile make thee to forget Bishops English, and weep Irish; next hanging, there is no better reuenge on Martin than to make him crie for anger; for there is no more sullen beast than a he drab. Ile make him pull his powting croscloath ouer his beetle browes for melancholie, and then my next booke shall be Martin in his mubble fubbles.

Here I was writing *Finis* and *Funis*, and determined to lay it by, till I might see more knauerie filde in: within a while appeared olde Martin with a wit worn into the socket, twinkling and pinking like the snuffe of a candle; *quantum mutatus ab illo*, how vnlike the knaue hee was before, not for malice but for sharpnesse.

[Pg 77]

The hogshead was euen come to the hauncing, and nothing could be drawne from him but dregs: yet the emptie caske sounds lowder than when it was ful; and protests more in his waining, than he could performe in his waxing. I drew neere the sillie soule, whom I found quiuering in two sheetes of protestation paper. O how meager and leane hee lookt, so creast falne, that his combe hung downe to his bill, and had I not been sure it was the picture of enuie, I shoulde haue sworne it had been the image of death, so like the verie Anatomie of mischiefe, that one might see through all the ribbes of his conscience, I began to crosse my selfe, and was readie to say the *Pater noster*, but that I knewe he carde not for it, and so vsed no other wordes, but *abi in malam crucem*, because I knewe, that lookt for him. I came so neere, that I could feele a substantiall knaue from a sprites shadowe.

I sawe through his paper coffen, that it was but a cosening corse, and one that had learnde of the holie maid of Kent, to lie in a trance, before he had brought foorth his lie; drawing his mouth awrie, that could neuer speake right; goggling with his eyes that watred with strong wine; licking his lips, and gaping, as though he should loose his childes nose, if he had not his longing to swallowe Churches; and swelling in the paunch, as though he had been in labour of a little babie, no bigger than rebellion; but [Pg 78] truth was at the

Bishoppes trauaile: so that Martin was deliuered by sedition, which pulls the monster with yron from the beastes bowells. When I perceiued that he masked in his rayling robes, I was so bolde as to pull off his shrowding sheete, that all the worlde might see the olde foole daunce naked.

Tis not a peniworth of protestation that can buy thy pardon, nor al worth a penie that thou proclaimest. Martin comes in with bloud, bloud, as though hee should bee a martir. Martins are mad martirs, some of them burnt seauen yeares agoe, and yet aliue. One of them lately at Yorke, pulling out his napkin to wipe his mouth after a lie, let drop a surgeans caliuer at his foote where he stood; these fellowes can abide no pompe, and yet you see they cannot be without a little squirting plate: rub no more, the curtall wrinches.

They call the Bishops butchers, I like the Metaphore wel, such calues must be knockt on the head, and who fitter than the Fathers of the Church to cut the throates of heresies in the Church. Nay, whē they haue no propertie of sheepe but bea, their fleece for flockes, not cloath, their rotten flesh for no dish, but ditches; I thinke them woorth neither the tarring nor the telling, but for their scabbednes to bee thrust from the pinfolde to the scaffold, and with an *Habeas corpus* to remooue them from the Shepheards tarre-boxe to the hangmans budget.

[Pg 79]

I but he hath sillogismes in pike sauce, and arguments that haue been these twentie yeres in pickle. I, picke hell, you shall not finde such reasons, they bee all in *celarent*, and dare not shewe their heads, for wee will answere them in *ferio* and cut their combes. So say they, their bloud is sought. Their bloud? What should wee doo with it, when it will make a dogge haue the toothach to eat the puddings.

Martin tunes his pipe to the lamentable note of *Ora whine meg*. O tis his best daunce next shaking of the sheetes; but hee good man meant no harme by it. No more did one of his minions, that thinking to rap out an oath and sweare by his conscience, mistooke the word and swore by his concupiscence; not vnlike the theefe, that in stead of God speede, sayd stand, and so tooke a purse for God morowe.

Yet dooth Martin hope that all her Maiesties best subiects will become Martinists; a blister of that tongue as bigge as a drummes head; for if the Queenes Maiestie haue such abiects for her best subiects, let all true subiects be accompted abiects.

They that teare the boughs, will hew at the tree, and hauing once wet their feete in factions, will not care how deep they wade in treason.

After Martin had racked ouer his protestation with a Iades pace, hee runnes ouer his fooleries with a knaues gallop, ripping vp the souterlie seames of his Epistle, botching in such frize iestes vppon fustion[Pg 80] earnest, that one seeing all sortes of his shreddes, would thinke he had robd a taylors shop boord; and then hee concludes all doggedlie, with Doctor *Bullens* dogge *Spring*, not remembring that there is not a better Spanniell in England to spring a couie of queanes than Martin.

Hee sliues one, has a fling at another, a long tale of his talboothe, of a vulnerall sermon, and of a fooles head in souce. This is the Epistle which he woonders at himselfe, and like an olde Ape, hugges the Vrchin so in his conceipt, as though it should shew vs some new tricks ouer the chaine, neuer wish it published Martin, we pittie it before it comes out. Trusse vp thy packet of flim flams and roage to some countrey Faire, or read it among boyes in the belfrie, neuer trouble the church with chattering; but if like dawes, you will be cawing about Churches, build your nests in the steeple, defile not the quier.

Martin writes merely, because (hee saies) people are carried away sooner with iest than earnest. I, but Martin neuer put Religion into a fooles coate; there is great oddes betweene a Gospeller and a Libeller.

If thy vaine bee so pleasaunt, and thy witt so nimble, that all consists in glicks and girds; pen some play for the Theater, write some ballads for blind *Dauid* and his boy, deuise some iests, and become another *Scogen*, so shalt thou haue vēt inough[Pg 81] for all thy vanities, thy Printer shall purchase, and all other iesters beg.

For to giue thee thy due, thou art the best died foole in graine that euer was, and all other fooles lacke manie graines, to make them so heauie.

There is not such a mad foole in Bedlam, nor such a baudie foole in Bridewell, nor such a dronken foole in the stockes, nor such a scolding foole on the cucking-stoole, nor such a cosening foole on the pillerie, nor such a roaging foole in the houses of correction, nor such a simple foole kept of alms, nor such a lame foole lying in the spittle, nor in all the world, such a foole, all. Nay for fooles set down in the scriptures, none such as Martin.

What atheist more foole, that saies in his heart, *There is no God*? What foole more proud, that stands in his own cōceit? What foole more couetous than he that seekes to tedd abroad the Churches goods with a forke, and scratch it to himselfe with a rake.

Thou seest Martin with a little helpe, to the foure and twentie orders of knaues, thou maist solder the foure and twentie orders of fooles, and so because thou saist thou art vnmarried, thou maist commit matrimonie, from the heires of whose incest, wee will say that which you cannot abide, *Good Lord deliuer vs*.

If this veyne bleede but six ounces more I shall[Pg 82] proue a pretie railer, and so in time may growe to bee a proper Martinist. Tush, I doo but licke ouer my pamphlet, like a Beares whelpe, to bring it in some forme; by that time he replies, it will haue clawes and teeth, and then let him looke to bee scratcht and bitten too.

Thou seest Martin Moldwarpe, that hetherto I haue named none, but markt them readie for the next market: if thou proceed in naming, be as sure as thy shirt to thy knaues skinne, that Ile name such, as though thou canst not blush, because thou art past shame, yet they shall bee sorie, because they are not all without grace.

Pasquil is coming out with the liues of the Saints. Beware my Comment, tis odds the margent shall be as full as the text. I haue manie sequences of Saints, if naming be the aduantage, and ripping vp of liues make sport; haue with thee knuckle deepe, it shall neuer bee said that I dare not venter mine eares where Martin hazards his necke.

Now me thinkes Martin begins to stretch himselfe like an old fencer, with a great conscience for buckler and a long tongue for a sword. Lie close, you old cutter at the locke, *Nam mihi sunt vires, et mea tela nocent*. Tis ods but that I shal thrust thee through the buckler into the brain, that is through the conscience into the wit.

If thou sue me for a double maime, I care not[Pg 83] though the Iurie allow thee treble damages, it cannot amount to much, because thy cōscience is without wit, and thy wit without conscience, and therefore both not worth a penie.

Therefore take this for the first venew, of a yonger brother, that meanes to drie beate those of the *Elder* house. Martin, this is my last straine for this fleech of mirth. I began with God morrowe, and bid you God night. I must tune my fiddle, and fetch some more rozen, that it maie squeake out Martins Matachine.

[Pg 84]

III.—NICHOLAS BRETON

(Wit and Will *has been already more frequently reprinted than most things of Breton's, but these reprints have been in very small numbers, and not generally accessible. It is given here as being equally characteristic of the author and of the time, both in matter and in form, in the mixture of verse and prose, in the plays on words, in the allegory, in the morality, and in the style.*)

THE WIL OF WIT, WIT'S WILL, OR WIL'S WIT, chuse you whether. Containing five discourses, the effects whereof follow. READE AND JUDGE. Compiled by NICHOLAS BRETON, gentleman. *Non hà, che non sà.* Vires sit Vulnere Veritas. London: Printed by THOMAS CREEDE, 1599.

[Pg 85]

TO GENTLMEN SCHOLLERS AND STUDENTS WHATSOEUER

Gentlemen, or others, who imploy your time in the studies of such Arts as are the ornaments of Gentilitie, to your courtesies I commend the vnlearned discourse of my little wit, which as I wil not intreate you to commend, deseruing the contrarie: so I hope you will not disdain, though it deserue discommendation, but so by your pardons excuse my small discretion by great desire, that hereafter, with less hast, I may take as great care as pains to publish a peece of worke somewhat more worth the perusing. Till when, wishing you all the fauor of God, with good fortune of the world, I rest in honour of learning to you and all students.

A LOUING FRIEND, N.B., GENTLEMAN.

THE EPISTLE TO THE GENTLE READER

A new booke says one; true, it came forth but tother day; good stuffe, says another. Read, then iudge. I confesse it may seeme to a number a bold attempt to set out a forme of wit, considering the witty discourses of such fine wits as haue deserued such comendation, as may driue this meane peece of woorke of mine into vtter disgrace, were it not that perfect courtesie dooth [Pg 86] bear with imperfect knowledge, regarding more the good minde in the writer then the matter written: and therefore the best will giue good words whatsoeuer they thinke, to encourage a forward wil to doo better, when indeed it were a fantasticall heade that could doo worse. Well when Wit is a wool-gathering, and Will wandring the world without guide, what a case that manne is in that is in such a taking; I referre you to mad folks of whom you may see examples suficient, and so I being in a certain melancholie moode past all Gods forbod, tooke my pen and Inke and Paper and somewhat I would go doo whatsoeuer it were to put out one conceit and bring in another. At last and at first of a suddaine warres and at adventures, by God's good helpe and good fortune the little wit that I had meeting with good Will, I knew not how, fell to worke (at first) I know not what, but hauing written a while, I made somewhat of it which, though little to any great purpose, yet if it please the Readers, I am contented, and if any man thinke it well done then Wit shall think Will a good boy, and Will shall think hee tooke Wit in a good vaine, and Will and Wit shall haue the more heart hereafter to fall to further woorke; but if I haue bin more wilful than wise to trouble your wittes with a witlesse peece of work pardon me for this once, ye shall see I will please you better hereafter; in the meane time desiring your courtesies to commend what you think worthie and not to disdain without desert, I rest wishing your content in what you wish well as I pray you wish me as I do you,

Your Friend Nicholas Breton, Gentleman.

[Pg 87]

AD LECTOREM, DE AUTHORE

What thing is Will, without good Wit?
Or what is Wit, without good Will?
The one the other doth so fit:
As each one can be but ill.
But when they once be well agreed,
Their worke is likely well to speed.

For proofe, behold good *Bretons* will,
By helpe of Wit, what it hath writ:
A worke not of the meanest skill,
Nor such as shewes a simple Wit.
But such a *wit* and such a *will*,
As hath done well, and hateth ill.

I need not to commend the man,
Whom none can justly discommend:
But do the best, the best that can,
Yet some will spite, and so I end.
What I have said, I say so still,
I must commend this Wit and Will.

FINIS

[Pg 88]

AD LECTOREM, DE AUTHORE

What shall I say of Gold, more then tis Gold:
Or call the Diamond, more then precious:
Or praise the man, with praises manifold
When of himselfe, himselfe is vertuous?
Wit is but *Wit*, yet such his *Wit* and *Will*,
As proues ill good, or makes good to be ill.

Why? what his *Wit*? proceed and aske his *Will*,
Why? what his *Will*? reade on, and learne of *Wit*:
Both good I gesse, yet each a seuerall ill,
This may seeme strange, to those that heare of it.
Nay, nere a whit, for vertue many waies,
Is made a vice, yet Vertue hath her praise.

Wherefore, O *Breton*, worthie is thy worke,
Of commendations worthie to the worth:
Sith captious wittes, in euerie corner lurke,
A bold attempt, it is to set them forth
A forme of Wit, and that in such a sort,
As none offends, for all is said in sport.

And such a sport, as serues for other kinds,
Both young and old, for learning, armes, and love:
For Ladies humors, mirth with mone he findes,
With some extreames, their patient mindes to proue.
Well, *Breton*, write in hand, thou hast the thing,
That when it comes, loue, wealth, and fame will bring.

W. S.

[Pg 89]

A PRETIE AND WITTIE DISCOURSE BETWIXT WIT AND WILL

Long have I travelled, much ground have I gone, many wayes have I trode, mickle mony have I spent, more labour have I lost, in seeking an olde friend of mine: whose companie so courteous, his counsaile commodious, his presence so pleasant, and his absence so greevous, that when I thinke of him, and misse him, I find such a misse of him, as all things are out of frame with me. And out of frame, can come to no good fashion. Oh, what shall I do? It is long since I lost him: long have I sought him. And too long (I fear) it wil be ere I find him. But wot you who it is? Oh, my Wit, I am from my Wit, and have bin long. Alas the day, I have bin almost mad with marching through the world without my good guide, my friend, and my companion, my brother, yea, my selfe. Alas, where is he? When shall I see him? How shall I seeke him, and whither shall I walke? I was too soone wearie of him, and am now wearie of my selfe without him. Well, I will go where I may, I may hap to find him: but hap is [Pg 90] unhappie. Therefore hap good, or hap ill, I will walke on still: if I find him, happie man. If I do not, what then? Content my selfe even as I can, patience where is no remedie.

Wit.

Long have I lookt, far have I sought, oft have I wisht, and sore have I longed for my merrie mate, my quicke sprite, my dearling, and my dearest byrd: Whose courtesie so contentive, whose helpe so necessary, whose necessitie so great, whose presence so pleased me, and absence so angers mee, that when I would have him, and see I am without him, I am not in order, and being out of order, can take no good course. Alas, what shall betide me? I have lost my love, or my love hath lost me. Would God wee might meete againe, and be merry togither: which I cannot bee without him? Oh, what have I lost? my Will, whither is he gone? when will he returne? who hath led him away? or will bring him backe againe? what company is he falne into? or how doth he leade his life? Well, time yet may turne him. Till when I wish for him, hoping to meete him, but hope is uncertaine;

Yet hope well, and have well,
Thus alone I cannot dwell;
If I find him so it is:
If not, then I wis,
[Pg 91] I must be content with this.
Patience is a vertue.
But whom doo I behold so neare?
It is my Will, with heavie cheere:

Well, I am sorie for this geare,
Yet will I to him out of hand,
And know, how so the case doth stand.
What? Will? *Will.* Who? Wit?

Wit. Whither away?

Will. Where I may.

Wit. Whereunto?

Will. Oh, to do.

Wit. What?

Will. Teach thou me that.

Wit. Why, sigh not, boy?

Will. Oh, all my joy.

Wit. Where is it, Will?

Will. Among the ill.

Wit. What, is it lost?

Will. That greeves me most.

Wit. And not to be recoverèd?

Will. Oh, my heart is almost dead.

Wit. What, Will, hold up head,
I will be thy friend to death.

Will. Then give me leave to fetch my breath,
And welcome: twise and thrice well met:
Where my hearts joy is set.
[Pg 92]Many a walk have I fet,
But no comfort could I get,
Till now by thee mine onely friend,
With whom I meane my life to end.
If thou wilt give me leave, good Wit.

Wit. Yes, good sweete Will, and glad of it.

Will. Then harke, good Wit, unto my tale:
Not of amidde my blisse in bale,
Nor any such like stuffe so stale.
I studie not to talke in verse,
But I will unto thee rehearse
A plaine discourse, in homely prose,
Wherein I will at large disclose:
How I have lived, with whom, and where:
How I was tossèd, here and there:
How I did chaunce to travaile hither,
And so we will be merrie togither.

Wit. Contented. Verse is good sometime,
But sometime prose, and sometime rime.
But be it either prose or verse,
What so thou wilt, good Will, rehearse:
I meane to heare it to the end,
And quit thee quickly as a friend.
But since thou likest prose so well,
Begin in prose thy tale to tell.

Willes Tale.

Oh, good Wit (if thou doost remember), I lost thee in travaile to the Well of Wisedome. Since[Pg 93] when, I have wandred through a wildernesse of woe, which in the Mappe of that Countrey (I find) is called the Desart of Desire. Wherein I saw so many wayes, as now in this, and then in that. At last I came to the hill of Hard Happe, which ledde mee downe into a Vale of Vanitie. There did I live in the Lake of Miseries, with the lost people, that having followed Fancie, found Penitence, the reward of running heads. But Lord what a life it is? I lothe to thinke on it. Beleeve mee, sweete Wit, there is such falling out with Fancie, who shifts all upon Folly. Such exclamation upon Folly, who brings them to Fortune: such cursing and banning of Fortune, for her froward dealing: in gentle helping them uppe uppon her wheele, and then suddaine dinging them downe (almost to their destruction), that if their bee a Hell in this world, there is the place. God keepe all good mindes from such a filthy corner. *Wit.* Amen. But tell me how camst thou thence? *Will.* I will tell you anon: but first I will tell you more. There is of all States. Princes crie out of cares: Lordes, of lacke of living: Ladyes, of false love: souldiers, of want of pay: Lawyers, of quiet: Poore men, of Lawe: Merchants, of shipwracke: Mariners, of fowle weather: Usurers, of sermons, and Divines, of usurie: Players, of Preachers, and Preachers, of Players: Dicers, of loosing, and losers, of dicing: Cryples, of fighting, and fighters, of hurts: the Rich, of sicknesse: the[Pg 94] Poore, of want: the Sicke, of paine: the healthfull, of ill happe: the unhappie, of the time that ever they were borne. Oh, it is a pittious crie: I would not be there againe, to heare it as I have done, for the gaine of Europe.

Wit. Beleeve me, I cannot blame thee: but tell me, how camst thou thence? *Will.* Oh, brother, I will tell you how: you know, sometime travellers must needes have rest, which they must come by as they may: Now, I having walked (as I told you) through this unpleasant place, weary at last, I laide mee downe in the ditch of Distresse: where, finding many dead sculles, and other boanes, I there thought to begin a sleepe, or sleepe my last: now lying there in such sort as I tell you, mee thought in my sleepe I sighed, in which sorrow a good motion of minde set my heart to prayer; which tended to this effect, that it would please the mightie and mercifull Majestie of the Most

Highest, to send me some meane, to lead me out of this miserie; beeing as it were from my Wit, and altogither comfortlesse. Now, suddenly there appeared unto me an olde aged man, who tooke me by the hand, with these words: Arise, thou sluggish wanton, walke no longer out of thy way, turne thee backe from this straie pathe, experience doth teach thee: What is Will without Wit? Prayer hath procured thee pardon, the high and onely God hath given thee Grace; by Grace goe seeke that is[Pg 95] worth the finding; look where Wit is; too him, and make much of him. With joy of that word, I awaked, and with shame of my folly in leaving thee, I hung the head; with sorrow whereof I was almost of life deprived; but now by thy sweete welcome wholy revived; now awake (I should say), I saw none but thee; and now, while I live, I will follow thee.

Wit. Why, was it heere you slept, or have you come farre since you waked? *Will.* No, no, heere did I sleepe, heere is the place of paine so unpleasant: but now I see thee, I have received comfort, for that I know thou canst leade me to Wisdome, who will soone shew me the way to paradise. *Wit.* Why then, Will, well hast thou slept, better hast thou dreamed, but best hast thou waked, to hit on mee so happily, who intend to bring thee to that good beginning, that shall leade thee to endlesse blisse. But to quit thy tale, I will tell thee a little of my travaile, and so we will away together.

Wits Tale.

Will, thou knowest when I left thee, in the lane of Learning, I went on straight to the schoole of Vertue, and with her Testimoniall, to the Well of Wisdome, which stands within the pallace of Patience; where I found the fountaine kept with foure ladies, whose names were Wisdome, Temperance, Fortitude, and Justice. Now, when I came thither, with sufficient[Pg 96] warning from Vertue, yet (for order sake) they thus used me; Wisedome, which stood with a snake in her hand (over whose head was written), *I see the holes that subtill serpents make*, thus used her warie speech unto me. Sirra (quoth she), how presume you into this place? from whence came you, and how and whither will you? Lady (quoth I), from Fancies forte I came, and am now travailing to the forte of Fame. I came now directly from the schoole of Vertue; brought thither by Learning had by Reason, servant to Instruction; and heere behold Patience, who hath lead me, who is further to plead for me. Welcome (quoth shee), but art thou not wearie? No (quoth I), nor would be, if the walke had beene longer, to have my will. *Will.* Why didst thou thinke me there abouts? Oh, lord, I was far wide. *Wit.* Peace, Will, a while: when I denide wearinesse; Yea (quoth Fortitude), an other of the Dames (over whose head was written, *I yield to good, but overthrow the ill*), I will see if you be wearie or not, I must trie a fall with you. At first I made no account of her, but when I begun, I found her of great force. Yet in the ende, shee was content to give me over, and let me come neare the Well. Now, upon the well brinkes stoode Justice, over whose head was written, *my hand hits right, death is my stroke, my ballance will not lye.* Then was my words written down by Memorie, and weyed with Truth; which being even in judgment,[Pg 97] shee bad me welcome, and so was content to let me lay my lips to the sweet lycquor of Sapience. Oh it is a delicate water!

Now, as I stoode, I heard a trumpet sound; which done, I heard a voyce which said: What trumpe can sound the true report of Fame? Now desirous to see the place, whence I heard this sound, I craved the ladies pasport to the said place, who gave me no other pasport than the commandement of Patience, warning me in any wise to take hold of Time, when I met him, and turne him to my use: with these two, I should come to the forte afore me. I, right glad of my good hap, tooke leave, and forth I went; anon I met Master Time, with his sithe in his hand, singing, *Save vertue, al things I cut downe, that stand within my way.* But as he came working, I watcht him neare, and as he strooke aside, I suddenly stept to him, tooke him by the noddle, and turned him to my work. What wouldest thou (quoth he)? I must not stand idle. No (quoth I), thou shalt walke, and leade me to the fort of Fame. Come, then (quoth he). Goe away softly (quoth Patience). Content (quoth I). And so togither we go to this stately Court; where, being first entertained by Courtly, we were brought to

Favour, and so led up to Fame. Now, being on knee before her highnesse, she first gave me her hand to kisse, and willed the lords to bid me welcome. See here (quoth she) the perfection[Pg 98] of affection, what a travaile he hath undertaken onely for our favour, which he shall be sure of. The Nobles used me honourably, the Gentlemen courteously, the Servants reverently, and Favour freendly. Now, as I stood, I heard such sweete musick, such heavenly songs, it made my heart leape to heare them. The prince did sing in praise of peace, the lords of plentie, the ladies of true love, the lawiers of quiet, the servaunts of lawe, the merchaunts of sayling, and saylers of faire weather, the rich of health, the poore of charitie, the healthfull of good happe, and the happie of Gods blessing: there was no usurers, dicers, players, nor fighters heard of. Oh, there was a place of pleasure; if in the world there be a paradice, that was it. Oh that thou haddest beene with mee!

Will. So would I, but tell me, how came you againe? *Wit.* I will tell thee. When I had beene within, and without, and heard such sweete harmony, of such singular musicke; at last, I came downe into the base court, led by Favour, to a lodging which was called the counting house; there sate Memorie, to take the names of such as had bin entertained, and meant to seeke favour, at the hands of happie Fame. But as I was going through the court, I met one of the maides of honour attendaunt upon the princesse, whose name (Favour told me) was Belezza, accompanied with Gentilezza, another of the maides. Now, as I was walking, I stared so earnestly on them, that[Pg 99] (not looking to my feete) I stumbled against a stone, and with the fall I awaked: now awake, I thought of my good Will; and see how soone it was my happe to meete with thee; but no sooner then I wished for thee, nor then I am heartily glad of thee. *Will.* Gramercy, Wit. But yet I beshrow thee. *Wit.* Why so? *Will.* For loosing mee. *Wit.* Thou mightest have followed. *Will.* You might have held me. *Wit.* When? *Will.* When I was neere you. *Wit.* Where was that?

Will. Where you lost me. But tell me one thing, where was it you slept, and awaked so sodainely? What? was it heere abouts? *Wit.* Yea, heere Will, heere, heere is the Forte of Fame, as thou shalt finde, when thou hast beene with me a while; there is no house, but hath a sinke; no field so fayre, but hath foule ditch; no place so pleasant, but hath a corner of anoyance; he that runnes retchlesly, falles headlong; and hee that is in a hole, he knowes not how, must come out he knowes not when. Care is to be had in all things, at all times, and in all places; well, thou hast knowne some sorrowe; learne to leave selfe judgement; follow friend, go with me. *Will.* Why? I would never have lost thee, but— *Wit.* But that thou wert wearie of me. *Will.* Why? I was not wearie, but— *Wit.* No, but that you were a wanton. *Will.* Why? I was not a wanton, but— *Wit.* No, but that you were wilfull. *Will.* Why? I was not wilfull,[Pg 100] but— *Wit.* No, but that you thought better of your selfe than any else. *Will.* Why? but I did not thinke so, but— *Wit.* Nay, you may say you would not have thought so, but—

Will. But what? or why? *Wit.* But because you did not see your selfe. *Will.* Yes, indeede, but I did; I did see my selfe and you too. *Wit.* Indeede, but you did not; for if you had seene me, you would not so have lost mee. *Will.* Yes, but I did see you, but when I had looked on you a while, I looked on my selfe so long, till you were out of sight, and then I looked after you and could not see you. *Wit.* Well, but then you sawe mee not, and so you lost mee; but since you now have found me, follow me neere, stay but a buts length behinde mee, least I suddainly steppe a flights shotte before you, and then a furlong further, you never overtake me. *Will.* But soft, runnes Wit so fast, Will is weerie. *Wit.* Goe too, throw off your clogge of care, trust to me, so you do as I bid you, all shall be well. *Will.* Yes, but— *Wit.* But what? *Will.* But a little of your helpe. *Wit.* Yes, but— *Will.* But? What? *Wit.* But that you must of your selfe labour. *Will.* So I will, but— *Wit.* But not too much: well, contented, I will worke. Wilt thou help? *Will.* Yea, willingly. *Wit.* How long? *Will.* Till death. *Wit.* Why, wilt thou dye? *Will.* Not with working: yet will I worke sore. *Wit.* Whereto? *Will.* To winne my wish.

[Pg 101]

Wit. What is that? *Will.* You can tell. *Wit.* But tell me. *Will.* What? *Wit.* Is it favour? *Will.* That is one parte of it. *Wit.* Wealth? *Will.* An other parte. *Wit.* Honour? *Will.* The greatest next. *Wit.* Content. *Will.* All in all. *Wit.* Where? *Will.* In heart. *Wit.* How? *Will.* By happe. *Wit.* How is that? *Will.* By hope. *Wit.* Oh, hope is vaine. *Will.* Oh, do not discomfort mee. *Wit.* Doubt the worst. *Will.* Wherefore? *Wit.* Because I bid thee. *Will.* Why doo you bid mee? *Wit.* For this reason: the best will helpe it selfe. *Will.* What is the worst? *Wit.* Envie. *Will.* What will hee doo? *Wit.* Mischiefe. *Will.* To whome? *Wit.* To good mindes. *Will.* How shall I doo, then? *Wit.* Let patience use prayer, God will preserve His servants.

Will. That I shall: then it is not impossible. *Wit.* What? *Will.* To get content? *Wit.* It is hard.

Will. What then? *Wit.* Doo our best. *Will.* Content. *Wit.* But harke, Will: shall I tell thee a little more of the fort of Fame, what I sawe and heard before I came away? Over the gate at the entrie, I sawe written pretie posies, some in Latine, some in Italian, some French, and some English. In Latine I remember these: *Quid tam difficile quod non solertia vincit?* By that was written, *Labore vertus*: and by that, *Vertute fama*: and over that, *Fama immortalis*: and that was written in many places [Pg 102] about the house. In Italian was written, *Gioventù vecchezza*: by that, *Vecchezza Morte, et Morte Tempo, et Tempo Fama*: but over all, *Sopra tutti, triumpha Iddio*. In French, *Le fol Fortune, il prudent Fame. Fame est divine, diuinitie est pretieuse, Dieu est nostre guarde.* In English was written. Patience is a vertue. Vertue is famous. Fame is divine. Divinitie is gratious. Grace is the gift of God: and God is the onely giver of grace. Which by patience seekes the vertue that is famous, to the divine pleasure of the Giver of all good gifts: blessed be His name, this shall he find, that enters the fort of Fame.

Will. Oh, sweete speeches. *Wit.* Then wil I tell thee further: as I walked up and down with Favour, I heard Courtesie and Content (a couple of courtiers) discoursing of thee and mee. Of the vertues of Wit, and the vanities of Will.

Wit, they sayde, was desirous of knowledge, but Will could take no paine: Wit would have patience, but Will would be wood with anger: Wit would worke, when Will would stand ydle: Wit would be walking, when Will would bee slouthfull: Wit woulde call for Willes helpe, when Will cared not for Wits counsaile: Wit woulde bee wise, and Will would be wanton: Wit would be vertuous, and Will vaine: Wit would be famous, and Will foolish: Wit would be sober, and Will frantick: Wit would be carefull, and Will carelesse: Wit studying, and Will playing: Wit at good[Pg 103] exercise, and Will idle, and worse occupied: Wit mourning for Will, Will making no mone for Wit: Wit in his dumps, and Will in delights: Wit would doo well, and have Will doo no worse, if he would follow him. But Will would loose Wit, and Wit must worke without Will and against Wit: and yet this is straunge, they were sworne brethren, one could not be without the other. Yet Wit could make better shift alone: Wit could finde Will, when he had lost himselfe, and Will (yet) would please Wit well, when he would be a good boy: which he would never be till he were beaten, and that with the smart of his owne rod: then he would come home to Wit, follow Wit as his best freend, and never leave him to the last houre.

Now when I heard this discourse I remembred thee, and beeing able to tarie no longer the hearing of such matter against him whom I love, I entreated Favour to bring me forth into the court, towardes the counting house: whither walking, I stumbled by the way, and fell as I told you: wherewith I awoke. Now, good Will, since I have found thee, and now thou seest the miseries of the world, come, followe me, let me bring thee to a better course: let not mee mourne for thee, nor other thus talke of thee: I will make much of thee, if thou wilt love mee: I will make thee give them cause to say: See what a chaunge! Will is come home, Will is content to be ruled by

Wit: hee workes with Wit, he walkes with [Pg 104] Wit: he mournes and is merie with Wit: he is travailing to Vertue with Wit, he will finde Fame by Wit: why he, Will? He is as welcome as Wit, as worthie as Wit, now he hath learned of Wit how to direct his course: beleeve me, Will, I love thee.

Will. Gramercie, good Wit, and I thee. But tell me one thing, mee thinks all this was but a dreame, for in the ende you did awake with the fall. *Wit.* True, Will, I was in a dreame, and so wert thou. *Will.* Oh, then, you did heare men talke so much of me in your sleepe: awake, I warrant you, you shall never heare so much amisse of me. *Wit.* I hope so too: now I have met with thee, I will shewe thee a way, whereby thou shalt deserve no such discredit. *Will.* Gramercie. But shall I now tell thee a little that I had forgotten, that I sawe and hearde in the Lake of Miserie? *Wit.* Contented, good Will, and gramercie too.

Will. Then, Wit, thou shalt understand, I heard these speeches past among penitent people: when Wit is wayward, Will is nobody: wofull Wit, blames wanton Will: wanton Wit, chides worthy Will: unhappie Wit, hasty Will: fantastical Wit, forward Will. Over that, Wit thinks scorne of Will, but yet he cannot bee without him: Wit hath lost Will, but yet he is glad to seeke him: Wit mournes for Will, but Wit sees it not: Will travailes for the stone, that Wit must whet himselfe uppon: Will is painefull, but [Pg 105] Wit unthankful: Will is courteous, but Wit curst: Will soone content, Wit too curious: Will would be ruled, but Wit had no reason: Will would have beene famous, had Wit beene vertuous: Will had beene good, had not Wit beene bad: Will had not lost Wit, had Wit lookt unto him: Will would doo well, if Wit would doo better: Will would learne, if Wit would teach him: but Will must worke without Wit, and against Wit: and yet it was woonderful that sworne brethren should so disagree, yet one so necessarie for the other in all actions, as nothing could hit well, when they were asunder. Will could meete Wit in a maze, and comfort him with his company: Will could bring Wit into a good order, when he was quite out of course. Wit would be glad of Will:

but when? When he found the want of his freend, which he would never doo, till he were wearie of working alone: and then he would embrace Will, make much of Will, and never leave Will for any worlds good. Now when I heard so much of my good Wit, I could not tarie any longer in the company, but from them I go, and by my selfe sate downe, where I slept, and awakt, as I told you.

Wit. Gramarcie, good Will; why then I perceive we were both asleepe, we lost one another in travaile, and travailed in sleepe, to seeke one another; which walking we have found: happy be this day of our meeting, and twise happy houre of this our freendly[Pg 106] greeting. Hee runs farre, that never turnes; hee turnes well, that stayes in time; and hee stayes well, that stands fast; he stands fast, that never falles; hee falles lowe, that never riseth; he riseth well, that stands alone when he is up. Good Will, well met, let us now bee merrie, shake hands, sweare company, and never part. *Will.* Content, heere is my hand, my heart is thine. But ere we goe any further, let us be a little merry. *Wit.* What shall we doo? *Will.* Let us sing. *Wit.* Content. But what? *Will.* What you will; begin, and I will answere you.

A Song betweene Wit and Will

Wit.	What	art	thou,	Will?
Will.	A	babe of	natures	brood.
Wit.	Who	was	thy	syre?
Will.	Sweet	lust,	as lovers	say.
Wit.		Thy	mother	who?
Will.	Wild	lustie	wanton	blood.
Wit.	When	wert	thou	borne?

Will. In merrie moneth of May.
Wit. And where brought up?
Will. In schoole of little skill.
Wit. What learndst thou there?
Will. Love is my Lesson still.

Wit. Where readst thou that?
[Pg 107]*Will.* In lines of sweete delight.
Wit. The author who?
Will. Desire did draw the booke.
Wit. Who teacheth? *Will.* Time.
Wit. What order? *Will.* Lovers right.
Wit. What's that? *Will.* To catch Content, by hooke or crooke.
Wit. Where keepes he schoole?
Will. In wildernesse of wo.
Wit. Why lives he there?
Will. The fates appoint it so.

Wit. Why did they so?

Will. It was their secret will.

Wit. What was their will?

Will. To worke fond lovers wo.

Wit. What was their woe?

Will. By spite their sport to spill.

Wit. What was their sport?

Will. Dame Nature best doth know.

Wit. How grows their spite?

Will. By want of wish.

Wit. What's that?

Will. Wit knowes right well, Will may not tell thee what.

Wit. Then, Will, adue.

Will. Yet stand me in some steed.

Wit. Wherewith, sweete Will?

Will. Alas, by thine advise.

Wit. Whereto, good Will?

Will. To win my wish with speed.

Wit. I know not how.

Will. Oh Lord, that Will were wise.

Wit. Wouldst thou be wise?

Will. Ful fain, then come from schoole.

Wit. Take this of Wit: Love learns to play the foole.

Will. Content, I wil come from Schoole, I wil give over *Artem Amandi*, and I will with thee to some more worthie study, which may be as well to my commoditie, comfort, as content. *Wit.* Well said, Will, now I like thee well; and, therefore, now I will do my best to worke thy delight. But for that now I have a peece of worke in hand, which none must be privie too, till it be finished; we will heere leave off talke, and fall to our worke togither, so I shall the sooner and the better dispatch it.

Will. Content, You shall have my helpe in it, or any other thing, wherein I may stand you in steed. And since you are so glad of my company, we will live and die togither. *Wit.* Gramercie, good Will; and meane time let us pray God to prosper our worke; let us have care how we worke; what, when, and where we worke, that we may find it commodious, not contrarie to Gods will, contentive to the best, offensive to fewe or none; let the matter be vertuous,[Pg 109] so shall he prove famous. *Will.* Good Wit, I thanke thee for thy good counsaile; God give us His grace to doo so. I am glad to see thee so well bent; now I must needs love thee; thou wert never wont to be so well minded. *Wit.* Better late than never; it is good to be honest, though a man had forsworne it; there is no time too late to thrive. *Will.* True; and I promise thee now, I hope I shall doo well by the comfortable counsaile of so good a friend. God be thanked, the old vaine is gone. *Stet pro ratione voluntas, Sum Juvenis fruar hoc mundo, Senex colam pietatem. Omnia vincit amor.* Faint heart never woon faire lady. Let us be merrie while we are here; when we are gone, all the world goes with us; let them take care that come after. A man is a man, if he have but a hose on his head. *Oh che bella donna? favor della Signora, oh dolce amore, La Sennora et spada, senza estos nada, Perle Amor de dieu: Beau damoiselle; oh brave huom; Che gallante cheval? il faut avoire come?* That makes no matter; then sweetes had no sower; but now Wit, oh Will, dost thou remember all this? I pray thee forget all, and think no more of such things. I am sorie that ever they were in my heart, but now thou shall see we will do well inough: we will take another way, to both our comforts. We will to Care, and intreate him to lend us his helpe, for without him, indeed we shall make an ilfavoured ende, of what we begin untowardly.[Pg 110] I promise thee, I heard the pretiest song betwixt him and Miserie that I heard a good while: if thou wilt set it downe in writing, I will recite it unto thee. *Wit.* Contented, right willingly, and thank thee too. *Will.* Then loe thus it was.

The Song betweene Miserie and Care.

M.	What		art		thou,	Care?
C.	A		secret		skil	unseene.
M.	Who		was		thy	syre?
C.	Sound	Wisdome.	*M.*	Mother		who?
C.	Devise.	*M.*	And	who	thy	nurse?
C.		Delight		I		weene.
M.	When		wert		thou	borne?

C. In harvest. *M.* What to do?

C. To worke? *M.* With whom?

C. With Wit and honest Will.

M. What worke? *C.* In graine, To gleane the good from ill.

M. What good? *C.* The best.

M. And how? *C.* By warie eye.

M. Whose eye is that?

C. The eye of perfect sight.

M. Who beares that eye?

C. The head that hath me nie.

M. Whose head is that?

[Pg 111]*C.* Each one that loves delight.

M. But what delight?

C. That longest doth endure.

M. Oh, Care. *C.* I come, Thy comfort to procure.

M. Whence dost thou come?

C. I come from loftie skie.

M. When camst thou thence?

C. Even now. *M.* Who sent thee so?

C. The gods. *M.* Whereto?

C. To comfort Miserie.

M. But how? *C.* By Wit. To worke his ease of wo.

M. What wo? *C.* The worst.

M. Whats that? *C.* The griefe of mind.

M. Oh. *C.* Feare not, Care Will quickly comfort find.

Wit. Beleeve me, I like it well: but is Care so comfortable: yea, indeed is it. Care is both a corsi[v]e and a comfort, all is in the use of it. Care is such a thing, as hath a great a doo in all things: why Care is a king in his kind. Did you never heare my discourse of Care in verse?

Will. No, that I remember: if it be not long, I pray you rehearse it. And for my better remembrance, henceforth, I will write it. *Wit.* Then give eare, thus it was.

[Pg 112]

THE SONG OF CARE

Come, all the world, submit your selves to Care,
And him acknowledge for your chiefest king:
With whom no King or Keisar may compare,
Who beares so great a sway in every thing.
At home, abroad, in peace, and eke in warre,
Care chiefly stands to either make or marre.

The court he keepes is in a wise conceit,
His house a head, where reason rules the wit:
His seate the heart that hateth all deceit,
His bed, the braine, that feels no frantick fit,
His diet is the cates of sweet content:
Thus is his life in heavenly pleasure spent.

His kingdome is the whole world round about,
Sorrow his sword, to such as do rebell:
His counsaile, wisedome, that decides each doubt,
His skill, foresight: of things to come, to tell.
His chiefe delight is studies of devise,
To keepe his subjects out of miseries.

Oh courteous king, oh high and mightie Care,
What shall I write in honour of thy name?
But to the world, by due desert declare
Thy royall state, and thy immortall fame.
Then so I end, as I at first begun,
Care is the king of kings, when all is done.

FINIS.

[Pg 113]

Will. Surely I never heard so much of Care before: but Reason hath shewed me, all is true that you have spoken of him. And therefore, let us humbly crave his helpe in this our worke which we are to take in hand, I dare warrant his favour. *Wit.* Sayest thou so, Will away, we have talked long: mountains never meete, but friends often: good happe comes oft unlookt for, but never unwelcome. I thought not to have found thee heere, but we see Fortune doth much, but Fates more, to bring friends togither: and friendship doth much, where faith is fixed: and faith is a jewell, and jewells are precious, and precious is for princes.

Oh God, trust me, Will, we must be warie to work, so with advise of Care, that as we are friends one to another, so we may prove in all actions to shew our cheefest jewell, our faithfull heart to God and her Majestie: to whom might we once be so happie as to presente a peece of worke worthy the receit: oh how glad shuld then our hearts be, which with faithful dutie would adventure death for her most excellent favour: which till by desert we find, and alwaies let us love and honour our singular good lord, that hath vouchsafed us his undeserved favour: and let us heartily pray for the preservation of her most excellent majestie, with long and prosperous raigne over us: as for the advancement of his honours estate, who by his vertues deserves, and by deserts[Pg 114] hath found favour of her highness, love of her peeres, honour of us, and a number our betters. And so let us away into my closset of Conceit, where from company we will thinke upon such matters as here wee will not talke on. *Will.* Content. We will go togither, studie thou, and I will make my pen, readie at thine, or his honors commandement. And thus till we have dispatcht our worke in hand, let us take our leave humbly of our good lord, and courteously of all our friends: Wishing them to employ their studies to the pleasure of God, content of the best sort, profit of themselves, and good example to others: and so *Bacciando le mani del Signore*, let us bid them all adiu. From our heart, this 8. of June, 1599.

INGENIJ VOLUNTAS.

[Pg 115]

IV.—ROBERT GREENE

(*One passage (that of the 'Shake-scene') in Greene's* Groat's Worth of Wit *has been hacked almost to death by the citations and discussions of Shakespearian commentators. But the rest has been but little referred to in comparison; and though it has been reprinted, it is not, to my knowledge, anywhere accessible as a whole, and is very generally unknown. It has, however, high interest, both external and internal, with the additional claim to preference over Greene's earlier euphuist romances and 'conny-catching' pamphlets that it is much shorter than the best of the former, and that nothing stands in the same relation to it as Dekker's* Hornbook *does to the latter. It wants little more introduction save the reminder that its autobiographic quality is evidently considerable in fact, if not so great as in intention, and that it was not printed till after the author's death.*)

GREENS,

Groats-worth of Wit,

bought with a Million of
Repentaunce.

Describing the follie of youth, the falshoode of makeshift flatterers, the miserie of the negligent, and mischiefes of deceiuing Courtezans.

Written before his death, and published at his
dying request.

Fœlicem fuisse infaustum.

Virescit vulnere veritas.

LONDON,
Printed by Thomas Creede, for Richard Oliue
dwelling in long Lane, and are there
to be solde. 1596.

[Pg 117]

THE PRINTER TO THE GENTLE READERS

I haue published heere Gentlemen for your mirth and benefit, *Greenes* groatesworth of wit. With sundry of his pleasant discourses, ye haue beene before delighted: But now hath death giuen a period to his pen: onely this happened into my hands, which I haue published for your pleasures: Accept it fauorably because it was his last birth, and not least worth, in my poore opinion. But I will cease to praise that which is aboue my conceit, and leaue it selfe to speake for it selfe: and so abide your learned censuring.

Yours, W. W./

TO THE GENTLEMEN READERS

GENTLEMEN. The Swan sings melodiously before death, that in all his life time vseth but a iarring sound. *Greene* though able inough to write, yet deeplyer searched with sickenesse than euer heretofore, sends you his Swanne-like song, for that he feares he shal neuer againe carroll [Pg 118] to you woonted loue layes, neuer againe discouer to you youths pleasures. How euer yet sickenesse, riot, incontinence, haue at once shown their extremitie, yet if I recouer, you shall all see more fresh springs, than euer sprang from me, directing you how to liue, yet not diswading you from loue. This is the last I haue writ, and I feare me the last I shall write. And how euer I haue beene censured for some of my former bookes, yet Gentlemen / I protest they were as I had speciall information. But passing them, I commend this to your fauorable censures, and like an Embrion without shape, I feare me will bee thrust into the world. If I liue to ende it, it shall be otherwise: if not, yet will I commend it to your courtesies, that you may as wel be acquainted with my repentant death, as you haue lamented my carelesse course of life. But as *Nemo ante obitum felix, so Acta Exitus probat*: Beseeching therefore to bee deemed hereof as I deserue, I leaue the worke to your likings, and leaue you to your delights./

[Pg 119]

A GROAT'S WORTH OF WIT

In an Iland bound with the Ocean, there was sometime a Citie situated, made rich by Marchandize and populous by long space: the name is not mentioned in the Antiquary, or else worne out by times Antiquitie: what it was it greatly skilles not: but therein thus it happened. An old new made Gentleman herein dwelt, of no small credit, exceeding wealth, and large conscience: he had gathered from many to bestowe vpon one, for though he had two sonnes, he esteemed but one, that being as himselfe, brought vp to be goldes bondman, was therefore held heire apparent of his ill gathered goods.

The other was a Scholler, and maried to a proper Gentlewoman, and therefore least regarded, for tis an olde said saw: To learning and law, ther's no greater foe, then they that nothing know: yet was not the father altogether vnlettered, for he had good experience in a *Nouerint*, and by the vniuersall tearmes therein contained, had driuen many gentlewomen to seeke vnknowen countries: wise he was, for he boare office in his / parish, and sate as formally [Pg 120] in his fox-furd gowne, as if he had beene a very vpright dealing Burges: he was religious too, neuer without a booke at his belt, and a bolt in his mouth, ready to shoote through his sinfull neighbor.

And Latin he had some where learned, which though it were but little, yet was it profitable, for he had this Philosophie written in a ring, *Tu tibi cura*, which precept he curiously obserued, being in selfeloue so religious, as he held it no point of charitie to part with any thing, of which he liuing might make vse.

But as all mortall things are momentarie, and no certaintie can bee founde in this vncertaine world, so *Gorinius* (for that shall be this Usurers name) after many a goutie pang that had pincht his exterior parts, many a curse of the people that mounted into heauens presence, was at last with his last summons, by a deadly disease arrested, where-against when hee had long contended, and was by Phisitions giuen ouer, hee cald his two sonnes before him: and willing to performe the olde prouerbe, *Qualis vita finis Ita*, hee thus prepared himselfe, and admonished them. My sonnes (for so your mother said ye were) and so I assure my selfe one of you is, and of the other I wil make no doubt.

You see the time is come, which I thought would neuer haue approached, and we must now be seperated, I feare neuer to meete againe. This sixteene[Pg 121] yeares daily haue I liued vexed with disease: and might I liue sixteene more, how euer miserably, I should thinke it happie. But death is relentlesse, and will not be intreated: witlesse, and knowes not what good my gold might do him: senseless, & hath no pleasure in the delightfull places / I would offer him. In breefe, I thinke he hath with this foole my eldest sonne beene brought vp in the vniuersitie, and therefore accounts that in riches is no vertue. But you my sonne (laying then his hand on the yongers head) haue thou another spirit: for without wealth life is a death: what is gentry if wealth be wanting, but base seruile beggerie? Some comfort yet it is vnto me, to see how many gallants sprung of noble parents haue croucht to *Gorinius* to haue sight of his gold: O gold, desired golde, admired golde! and haue lost their patrimonies to *Gorinius*, because they haue not returned by their day that adored creature! How many schollers haue written rimes in *Gorinius* praise, and receiued (after long capping and reuerence) a sixpeny reward in signe of my superficiall liberalitie. Breefely my yong *Lucanio*, how I haue bin reuerenst thou seest, when honester men I confesse, haue beene set farre off: for to be rich is to be any thing, wise, honest, worshipfull, or what not? I tell thee my sonne: when I came first to this Cittie, my whole wardrop was onely a sute of white sheepe skins, my wealth an olde Groate, my wooning,[Pg 122] the wide world. At this instant (O griefe to part with it) I haue in readie coyne threescore thousand pound, in plate and Jewels, xv. thousand, in bonds and specialties as much, in land nine hundred pound by the yeere: all which, *Lucanio* I bequeath to thee, onely I reserue for *Roberto* thy well red brother, an olde Groate (being the stocke I first began with) wherewith I wish him to buy a groatsworth of wit: for he in my life hath reprooued my maner of life, and therefore at my death, shall not be contaminated with corrupt gaine. Heere by the way Gentlemen must I disgresse to shew the reason of *Gorinius* present speech: *Roberto* being / come from the Academie, to visit his father, there was a great feast prouided: where for table talke, *Roberto* knowing his father and most of the companie to be execrable vsurers, inuayed mightily against that abhorred vice, insomuch that he vrged teares from diuers of their eyes, and compunction in some of their hearts. Dinner being past, hee comes to his father, requesting him to take no offence at his liberall speech, seeing what he had vttered was truth. Angrie, sonne (saide he) no by my honesty (& that is somwhat I may say to you), but vse it still, and if thou canst perswade any of my neighbours from lending vppon vsurie, I should haue the more customers: to which when *Roberto* would haue replied, he shut himselfe into his studie, and fell to telling ouer his money.

[Pg 123]

This was *Robertos* offence: nowe returne we to seeke *Gorinius*, who after he had thus vnequally distributed his goods and possessions, began to aske his sons how they liked his bequestes: either seemed agreed, and *Roberto* vrged him with nothing more, then repentance of his sin: Loke to thine owne, said he, fond boy, and come my *Lucanio*, let me giue thee good counsel before my death: as for you sir, your bookes are your counsellors, and therefore to them I bequeath you. Ah *Lucanio*, my onely comfort, because I hope thou wilt as thy father be a gatherer, let me blesse thee before I die. Multiply in wealth my sonne by anie meanes thou maist, onely flie Alchymie, for therein are more deceites then her beggerly Artistes haue wordes; and yet are the wretches more talkatiue then women. But my meaning is, thou shouldest not stand on conscience in causes of profite, but heape treasure vpon treasure, for the time of neede: yet seeme / to be deuout, else shalt thou be held vile: frequent holy exercises, graue companie, and aboue all, vse the conuersation of yong Gentlemen, who are so wedded to prodigalitie, that once in a quarter necessity knocks at their chamber doores: profer them kindnesse to relieue their wants, but be sure of good assurance: giue faire words till dayes of payment come, and then vse my course, spare none: what though they tell of conscience (as a number will talke) looke but[Pg 124] into the dealings of the world, & thou shalt see it is but idle words. Seest thou not many perish in the streetes, and fall to theft for neede: whom small succor would releeue. Then where is conscience, and why art thou bound to vse it more then other men? Seest thou not daily forgeries, periuries, oppressions, rackings of the poore, raysing of rents, inhauncing of duties, euen by them that shuld be all conscience, if they meant as they speake: but *Lucanio* if thou reade well this booke, (and with that hee reacht him Machiauels works at large) thou shalt see what it is to be fooleholy, as to make scruple of conscience, where profit presents it selfe.

Besides, thou hast an instance by thy threed-bare brother heere, who willing to do no wrong, hath lost his childs right: for who would wish any thing to him, that knowes not how to vse it?

So much *Lucanio* for conscience: and yet I knowe not whats the reason, but somewhat stings mee inwardly when I speake of it. I, father, said *Roberto*, it is the worme of conscience, that vrges you at the last houre to remember your life, that eternall life may follow your repentance. Out foole (said this miserable father) I feele it now, it was onely a stitch. I will forward with my exhortation to *Lucanio*. As I saide my / sonne, make spoyle of yong gallants by insinuating thy selfe amongst them, and be not mooued to think their Auncestors were famous, but[Pg 125] consider thine were obscure, and that thy father was the first Gentleman of the name: *Lucanio* thou art yet a Bachelor, and so keepe thee, till thou meete with one that is thy equall, I meane in wealth: regard not beautie, it is but a baite to entice thine neighbors eie: and the most faire are commonly most fond: vse not too many familiars, for few prooue friends, and as easie it is to weigh the wind, as to diue into the thoughts of worldly glosers. I tell thee *Lucanio*, I haue seene foure score winters besides the odde seauen, yet saw I neuer him that I esteemed as my friend but gold, that desired creature, whom I haue deerely loued, and found so firme a friend, as nothing, to me hauing it, hath beene wanting. No man but may thinke deerely of a true friend, and so doe I of it, laying it vnder sure locks, and lodging my heart therwith.

But now (Ah my *Lucanio*) now must I leaue it, and to thee I leaue it with this lesson, loue none but thy selfe, if thou wilt liue esteemed. So turning him to his study, where his chiefe treasure lay, he loud cried out in the wise mans words, *O mors quam amara,* O death how bitter is thy memorie to him that hath al pleasures in this life, and so with two or three lamentable groanes he left his life: and to make short worke, was by *Lucanio* his sonne enterd, as the custome is with some solemnitie: But leauing him that hath left the world to [Pg 126]him y^t censureth of euery worldly man, passe we to his sons: and see how his long laied vp store is by *Lucanio* looked into. The youth was of cōdition simple, shamefast, and flexible to any counsaile, which *Roberto* perceiuing, and pondering how little was left to him, grew into an inward contempt of his fathers vnequall legacie, and determinate resolution to worke *Lucanio* al possible iniurie: here vpon thus conuerting the sweetnesse of his studie to the sharpe thirst of reuenge, he (as Enuie is seldome idle) sought out fit companions to effect his unbrotherly resolution. Neither in such a case is ill companie farre to seeke, for the Sea hath scarce so ioperdies, as populous Citties haue deceiuing Syrens, whose eies are Adamants, whose wares are witchcrafts, whose doores leade downe to death. With one of these female Serpents *Roberto* consorts, and they conclude, what euer they compassed, equally to share to their contentes. This match made, *Lucanio* was by his brother brought to the bush, where he had scarce pruned his wings but hee was fast limed, and *Roberto* had what he expected. But that we may keepe forme, you shall heare how it fortuned.

Lucanio being on a time very pensiue, his brother brake with him in these tearmes. I wonder *Lucanio* why you are so disconsolate, that want not any thing in the world that may worke your content. If wealth may delight a man, you are with that suffi[Pg 127]ciently furnisht: if credit may procure a man any comfort, your word I knowe well, is as well accepted as any mans obligation: in this Citie are faire buildings and pleasant gardens, and cause of solace: of them I am assured you haue your choyse. Consider brother you are yong, then plod not altogether in meditating on our fathers precepts: which howsoeuer they sauoured of profit, were most vnsauerly to one of your yeeres applied. You must not thinke but certaine Marchants of this Citie expect your company, sundry Gentlemen desire your / familiarity, and by conuersing with such, you will be accounted a Gentleman: otherwise a pesant, if ye liue thus obscurely. Besides, which I had almost forgot, and then had all the rest beene nothing, you are a man by nature furnished with all exquisite proportion, worthy the loue of any courtly Ladie, be she neuer so amorous: you haue wealth to maintaine her, of women not little longed for: wordes to court her you shall not want, for my selfe will be your secretary. Brieflie, why stande I to distinguish abilitie in perticularities, when in one word it may be sayde, which no man can gainsay, *Lucanio* lacketh nothing to delight a wife, nor any thing but a wife to delight him? My young maister beeing thus clawde, and puft vp with his owne prayse, made no longer delay, but hauing on his holyday hose, he tricked himselfe vp, and like a fellowe that meant good sooth, hee[Pg 128] clapped his Brother on the Shoulder, and sayde. Faith Brother *Roberto*, and yee say the worde, lets go seeke a wife while it is hote, both of vs togither. Ile pay well, and I dare turne you loose to say as well as anye of them all: well Ile doe my best, said *Roberto*, and since ye are so forward, lets goe nowe and trie our good fortune.

With this foorth they walke, and *Roberto* went directlie towarde the house where *Lamilia* (for so wee call the Curtezan) kept her Hospital, which was in the Suburbes of the Cittie, pleasauntly seated, and made more delectable by a pleasaunt Garden, wherein it was scituate. No sooner come they within ken, but Mistresse *Lamilia* like a cunning angler made readie her chaunge of baytes, that shee might effect *Lucanios* bane: and to begin, shee discouered from her window her beauteous inticing face, and taking a lute in her hād that / she might the rather allure, she sung this Sonnet with a delicious voice.

Lamilias Song.

Fie fie on blind fancie,
It hinders youths ioy:
Faire virgins learne by me,
To count loue a toy.

When Loue learned first the A B C of delight,
And knew no figures, nor conceited phrase:
He simplie gaue to due desert her right,
He led not louers in darke winding wayes:
[Pg 129] He plainly wild to loue, or flatly answered no,
But now who lists to proue, shall find it nothing so:
Fie fie then on fancie,
It hinders youths ioy,
Faire virgins learne by me,
To count loue a toy.
For since he learnd to vse the Poets pen,
He learnd likewise with smoothing words to faine,
Witching chast eares with trothlesse toungs of men,
And wrayed faith with falshood and disdaine.

He giues a promise now, anon he sweareth no,
Who lifteth for to proue, shall find his changings so:
Fie fie then on fancie
It hinders youth[s] ioy,
Faire virgins learn by me,
To count loue a toy.

While this painted sepulchre was shadowing her corrupting guilt, Hiena-like alluring to destruction, *Roberto* and *Lucanio* vnder the windowe, kept euen pace with / euery stop of her instrument, but especially my yong Ruffler (that before time like a bird in a cage, had beene prentise for three liues or one and twentie yeeres at least, to esteame Auarice his deceased father). O twas a world to see how he sometime simperd it, striuing to set a countenance on his turnd face, that it might seeme of wainscot proofe, to beholde her face without blushing: anone he would stroake his bow-bent-leg, as though he went to shoote loue arrows from his shins: then wipte his chin (for his beard was not yet grown) with a gold [Pg 130] wrought handkercher, whence of purpose he let fall a handfull of angels. This golden showre was no sooner rained, but *Lamil[i]a*, ceast her song, and *Roberto* (assuring himselfe the foole was caught) came to *Lucanio* (that stoode now as one that had starde *Medusa* in the face) and awaked him from his amazement with these words: What, in a traunce brother? whence springs these dumps? are yee amazed at this obiect? or long ye to become loues subiect? Is there not difference betweene this delectable life and the imprisonment you haue all your life hitherto endured? If the sight and hearing of this harmonious beautie work in you effects of wonder, what will the possession of so diuine an essence, wherein beautie and Art dwell in their perfect excellencie. Brother said *Lucanio*, lets vse few words, and she be no more then a woman, I trust youle helpe mee to her? and if you doe, well, I say no more, but I am yours till death vs depart, and what is mine shal ye yours, world without end, Amen.

Roberto smiling at his simplenesse, helpt him to gather vp his dropt golde, and without any more circumstance led him to *Lamilias* house: for of such places it may be said as of hell. /

Noctes atque dies patet atri ianua ditis.

So their doores are euer open to entice youth[Pg 131] to destruction. They were no sooner entred, but *Lamilia* her selfe, like a second *Helen*, court-like begins to salute *Roberto*, yet did her wandring eie glance often at *Lucanio*: the effect of her entertainment consisted in these tearmes, that to her simple house Signor *Roberto* was welcome, and his brother the better welcome for your sake: albeit his good report confirmed by his present demeaner, were of it selfe enough to giue him deserued entertainement, in any place how honourable soeuer: mutuall thanks returned, they lead this prodigal childe into a Parlor, garnished with goodly portratures of amiable personages: neere which, an excellent consert of musicke began at their entrance to play. *Lamilia* seeing *Lucanio* shamefast, tooke him by the hand, and tenderly wringing him, vsed these words: Beleeue me Gentlemen, I am verie sorie that our rude enter[tain]ment is such, as no way may worke your content: for this I haue noted since your first entering, that your countenance hath beene heauie, and the face being the glasse of the heart, assures me the same is not quiet: would ye wish any thing heere that might content you, say but the word, and assure ye of present deliuerance to effect your full delight. *Lucanio* being so farre in loue, as he perswaded himselfe without her grant hee could not liue, had a good meaning to vtter his minde, but wanting fit wordes, hee stoode like a trewant that lackt a[Pg 132] prompter, or a plaier that being out of his part at his first entrance is faine to haue the booke to speake what he should performe. Which *Roberto* perceiuing replied thus in his behalfe: Madame, the Sunnes brightnesse daisleth the beholders eies, the maiestie of Gods, / amazed humane men. *Tullie* Prince of Orators, once fainted though his cause were good, and he that tamed monsters, stoode amated at beauties ornaments: Then blame not this yoong man though hee replied not, for he is blinded with the beautie of your sunne-darkening eies, made mute with the celestiall organe of your voyce, and feare of that rich ambush of amber colored darts, whose pointes are leuelde against his heart. Well Signor *Roberto* saide shee, how euer you interpret their sharpe leuell, be sure they are not bent to doe him hurt, and but that modestie blindes vs poore Maidens from vttering the inwarde sorrowe of our mindes, perchaunce the cause of greefe is ours, how euer men do colour, for as I am a virgin I protest (and therewithall shee tainted her cheekes with a vermilion blush) I neuer sawe Gentleman in my life in my eie so gratious as is *Lucanio*, onely that is my greefe, that either I am despised for that he scornes to speake, or else (which is my greater sorrow) I feare he cannot speake. Not speake Gentlewoman quoth *Lucanio*? that were a ieast indeede: yes, I thanke God I am sounde of winde and lim, onely[Pg 133] my heart is not as it was woont: but and you be as good as your word, that will soone be well, and so crauing ye of more acquaintance, in token of my plaine meaning receiue this diamond, which my olde father loued deerely: and with that deliuered her a Ring, wherein was apointed a Diamond of wonderfull worth. Which shee accepting with a lowe conge, returned him a silke Riband for a fauour, tyed with a truelouers knot, which he fastened vnder a faire Jewell on his Beuer felt.

After this *Diomedis & Glauci permutatio*, my young master / waxed cranke, and the musicke continuing, was very forward in dauncing, to shew his cunning: and so desiring them to play on a hornepipe, laid on the pauement lustily with his leaden heeles, coruetting like a steede of *Signor Roccoes* teaching, and wanted nothing but bels, to bee a hobbyhorse in a morrice. Yet was he soothed in his folly, and what euer he did, *Lamilia* counted excellent: her praise made him proude, insomuch that if he had not beene intreated, hee would rather haue died in his daunce, then left off to shew his mistresse delight. At last reasonably perswaded, seeing the table furnished, he was contented to cease, and settle himselfe to his victuals, on which (hauing before labored) he fed lustily, especially of a Woodcocke pie, wherewith *Lamilia* his caruer, plentifully plied him. Full dishes hauing furnisht emptie[Pg 134] stomaches, and *Lucanio* thereby got leisure to talke, falles to discourse of his wealth, his lands, his bonds, his abilitie, and how himselfe with all he had, was at Madame *Lamilias* disposing: desiring her afore his brother, to tell him simply what shee meant. *Lamilia* replied: My sweet *Lucanio*, how I esteeme of thee mine eies doe witnesse, that like handmaides, haue attended thy beautious face, euer since I first beheld thee: yet seeing loue that lasteth gathereth by degrees his liking, let this for that suffice: if I finde thee firme, *Lamilia* will be faithful: if fleeting, she must of necessitie be infortunate that hauing neuer seene any whome before shee could affect, shee shoulde bee of him iniuriously forsaken. Nay saide *Lucanio*, I dare say my brother here will giue his word. For that I accept your own said *Lamilia*, for with me your credit is better then your brothers. *Roberto* brake off their amorous prattle with these speeches. Sith / either of you are of other so fond at the first sight, I doubt not but time will make your loue more firme. Yet madame *Lamilia* although my brother and you be thus forward, some crosse chaunce may come: for *Multa cadunt inter calicem supremaq. labra*. And for a warning to teach you both wit, Ile tell you an olde wiues tale.

Before ye go on with your tale (quoth mistresse *Lamilia*) let me giue ye a caueat by the way, which shall be figured in a Fable.

[Pg 135]

Lamiliaes Tale.

The Foxe on a time came to visite the Gray, partly for kindered, cheefely for craft: and finding the hole emptie of all other companie, sauing onely one Badger; enquiring the cause of his solitarinesse, he described the sodaine death of his dam and sire, with the rest of his consorts. The Foxe made a Friday face, counterfeiting sorrow: but concluding that deaths shake was vneuitable, perswaded him to seeke some fit mate wherwith to match. The Badger soone agreed: so forth they went, and in their way met with a wanton ewe straggling from the fold: the Foxe bad the Badger play the tall stripling, and strout on his tiptoes: for (quoth he) this ewe is lady of al these lands, and her brother cheefe bel-weather of sundrie flocks. To be short, by the Foxes permission there would be a perpetuall league betweene her harmelesse kindred and al other deuouring beasts, for that the Badger was to them all allied: seduced, shee yeelded: and the Foxe conducted them to the Badgers / habitation, where drawing her aside vnder color of exhortation, [he] pulde out her throate to satisfie his greedie thurst. Here I should note, a yoong whelpe that viewed their walke, infourmed the shepheard of what hapned. They followed, and trained the Foxe and Badger to the hole: the Foxe afore had craftily conuaied him[Pg 136]self away: the shepheard found the Badger rauing for the ewes murther: his lamentation being helde for counterfet, was by the shepheards dog wearied. The Foxe escaped: the ewe was spoiled: and euer since, betweene the Badgers and the dogges, hath continued a mortall enmitie: And now be aduised *Roberto* (quoth she), goe forward with your tale, seeke not by slie insinuation to turne our mirth to sorrow. Go too *Lamilia* (quoth hee), you feare what I meane not, but how euer ye take it, Ile forward with my tale.

Robertoes Tale.

In the North parts there dwelt an old Squier, that had a yong daughter his heire; who had (as I know Madame *Lamilia* you haue had) many youthfull Gentlemen that long time sued to obtaine her loue. But she knowing her owne perfection (as women are by nature proude) woulde not to any of them vouchsafe fauour: insomuch that they perceiuing her relentlesse, shewed themselues not altogether witlesse, but left her to her fortune, when they founde her frowardnesse. At last it fortuned among other strangers, a Farmers sonne visited her fathers house: on whom at the first sight shee was enamored, he likewise on hir. Tokens of loue past betweene them, either acquainted others parents of their choise, and they kindly gaue their consent. Short tale to make, married they were, and great solemnitie was[Pg 137] at the wedding feast. A yong Gentleman, that had beene long a suter to her, vexing that the sonne of a farmer should be so preferred, cast in his minde by what meanes (to marre their merriment) he might steale away the Bride. Hereupon he confers with an old beldam, called mother *Gunby*, dwelling thereby, whose counsell hauing taken, he fell to his practise, and proceeded thus. In the after noone, when dauncers were very busie, he takes the Bride by the hand, and after a turne or two, tels her in her eare, he had a secret to impart vnto her, appointing her in any wise, in the euening to find a time to confer with him: she promised she would and so they parted. Then goes he to the bridegroome, and with protestations of entire affect, protests that the great sorrow hee takes at that which he must vtter, whereon depended his especial credit, if it were knowne the matter by him should be discouered. After the bridegroomes promise of secrecie, the gentleman tels him, that a friend of his receiued that morning from ye bride a letter, wherein she willed him with some sixteene horse to awaite her comming at a Parke side, for that she detested him in her heart as a base country hinde, with whom her father compelled her to marrie. The bridegroome almost out of his wits, began to bite his lippe. Nay, saith the Gentleman, if you will by me be aduised, you shall saue her credit, win her by kindnes, and yet preuent her[Pg 138] wanton complot. As how, said the Bridegroome? Mary, thus, said the gentleman: In the euening (for till the guests be gone she intends not to gad) get you / on horsebacke, and seeme to be of the companie that attends her comming: I am appointed to bring her from the house to the Parke, and from thence fetch a winding compasse of a mile about, but to turne vnto olde mother *Gunbyes* house, where her louer my friend abides: when she alights, I wil conduct her to a chamber far from his lodging, but when the lights are out, and she expects her adulterous copesmate, your selfe (as reason is) shall proue her bedfellow, where priuately you may reprooue her, and in the morning earely returne home without trouble. As for the gentleman my frend, I will excuse her absence to him, by saying, shee mockt thee with her maide in stead of her selfe, whom when I knew at her lighting, I disdained to bring her vnto his presence. The Bridegroome gaue his hand it should be so.

Now by the way we must vnderstand this mother *Gunby* had a daughter, who all that day sate heauily at home with a willow garland, for that the bridegroome (if he had dealt faithfully) should haue wedded her before any other. But men (*Lamilia*) are vnconstant, mony now a daies makes the match, or else the match is marde.

But to the matter: the bride groome and the Gentleman thus agreed: he tooke his time, conferred with the bride, perswaded her that her husband (notwithstanding his faire shew at the marriage) had sworne to his old sweete heart, their neighbour *Gunbyes* daughter, to be that night her bedfellow: and if she would bring her father, his father, and other friends to the house at midnight, they should finde it so.

At this the yong gentlewoman inwardly vext to be by a peasant so abused, promised if she sawe likelyhood of / his slipping away, that then she would doe according as he directed.

All this thus sorting, the old womans daughter was trickly attired, ready to furnish this pageant, for her old mother promised all things necessarie.

Well, Supper past, dauncing ended, all the guests would home, and the Bridgroome pretending to bring some friend of his home, got his horse, and to the Parke side he rode, and stayed with the horsemen that attended the Gentleman.

Anone came *Marian* like mistris Bride, and mounted behind the gentleman, away they post, fetch their compasse, & at last alight at an olde wiues house, where sodenly she is conuaied to her chamber, & the bridegroome sent to keepe her company: where he had scarce deuised how to begin his exhortation, but the father of his bride knockt at the chamber doore. At which being somewhat amazed, yet thinking to turne it to a ieast, sith his wife (as he thought) was in bed with him, hee opened the doore, saying: Father, you are heartily welcome, I wonder how you found vs out heere; this deuise to remooue our selues, was with my wiues consent, that we might rest quietly without the Maids and Batchelers disturbing vs. But where is your wife said ye gentleman? why heere in bed said he. I thought (quoth the other) my daughter had beene your wife, for sure I am to-day shee was giuen you in marriage. You are merrily disposed said the Bridegroome, what, thinke you I haue another wife? I thinke but as you speake, quoth the gentleman, for my daughter is below, & you say your wife is in the bed. Below (said he) you are a merie man, and with that casting on a night-gowne, he went downe, where when he saw his wife, the gentleman his father, and a number / of his friends assembled, he was so confounded, that how to behaue himselfe he knew not; onely hee cried out that he was deceiued. At this the olde woman arises, and making her selfe ignorant of al the whole matter, enquires the cause of that sodaine tumult. When she was tolde the new bridegroome was found in bed with her daughter, she exclaimed against so great an iniurie. *Marian* was called in quorum: she iustified it was by his allurement: he being condemned by al their consents, was iudged vnworthy to haue the gentlewoman vnto his wife, & compelled (for escaping of punishment) to marrie *Marian*: and the yong Gentleman (for his care in discouering the farmers sonnes leudnes) was recompenst with the Gentlewomans euer during loue.

Quoth *Lamilia*, and what of this? Nay nothing saide *Roberto*, but that I haue told you the effects of sodaine loue: yet the best is, my brother is a maidenly batcheler, and for your selfe, you haue beene troubled with many suters. The fewer the better, said *Lucanio*. But brother, I con you little thanke for this tale: hereafter I pray you vse other table talke. Lets then end talk, quoth *Lamilia*, and you (signor *Lucanio*) and I will goe to the Chesse. To Chesse, said he, what meane you by that? It is a game, said she, that the first danger is but a checke, the worst, the giuing of a mate. Wel, said *Roberto*, that game ye haue beene at alreadie then, for you checkt him first with your beauty, & gaue your self for mate to him by your bountie. That is wel taken brother, said *Lucanio*, so haue we past our game at

Chesse. Wil ye play at tables then, said she? I cannot, quoth he, for I can goe no furder with my game, if I be once taken. Will ye play then at cards? I, said he, if it be at one and thirtie. That fooles game, said she? Weele all to hazard, said *Roberto*, and / brother you shall make one for an houre or two: contented quoth he. So to dice they went, and fortune so fauoured *Lucanio*, that while they [Pg 142] continued square play, he was no looser. Anone cosonage came about, and his Angels being double winged flew cleane from before him. *Lamilia* being the winner, prepared a banquet; which finished, *Roberto* aduised his brother to depart home, and to furnish himselfe with more crownes, least he were outcrakt with new commers.

Lucanio loath to be outcountenanst, followed his aduise, desiring to attend his returne, which he before had determined vnrequested: for as soone as his brothers backe was turned, *Roberto* begins to reckon with *Lamilia*, to bee a sharer as well in the mony deceitfully woone, as in the Diamond so wilfully giuen. But she, *secundum mores meretricis*, iested thus with the scholler. Why *Roberto*, are you so well read, and yet shew your selfe so shallow witted, to deeme women so weake of conceit, that they see not into mens demerites? Suppose (to make you my stale to catch the woodcocke, your brother) that my tongue ouerrunning mine intent, I spake of liberal rewarde; but what I promised, there is the point; at least what I part with, I will be well aduised. It may be you wil thus reason: Had not *Roberto* trained *Lucanio* with *Lamilias* lure, *Lucanio* had not now beene *Lamilias* prey: therfore sith by *Roberto* she possesseth her prize, *Roberto* merites an equall part. Monstrous absurd if so you reason; as wel you may reason thus: *Lamilias* dog hath kilde [Pg 143] her a deere, therefore his mistris must make him a pastie. No poore pennilesse Poet, thou art beguilde in me, and yet I wonder how thou couldest, thou hast beene so often beguilde. But it fareth with licentious men, as with the chased bore in the / streame, who being greatly refreshed with swimming, neuer feeleth any smart vntill he perish recurelesly wounded with his owne weapons. Reasonlesse *Roberto*, that hauing but a brokers place, asked a lenders rewarde. Faithlesse *Roberto*, that hast attempted to betray thy brother, irreligiously forsaken thy wife, deseruedly beene in thy fathers eie an abiect: thinkest thou *Lamilia* so loose, to consort with one so lewd? No hypocrite, the sweete Gentleman thy brother, I will till death loue, and thee while I liue loath. This share *Lamilia* giues thee, other gettest thou none.

As *Roberto* would haue replied, *Lucanio* approached: to whom *Lamilia* discourst the whole deceit of his brother, & neuer rested intimating malitious arguments, till *Lucanio* vtterly refused *Roberto* for his brother, and for euer forbad him of his house. And when he wold haue yeelded reasons, and formed excuse, *Lucanios* impatience (vrged by her importunate malice) forbad all reasoning with them that was reasonlesse, and so giuing him Jacke Drums entertainment, shut him out of doores: whom we will follow, and leaue *Lucanio* to the mercie of[Pg 144] *Lamilia*. *Roberto* in an extreame extasie rent his haire, curst his destinie, blamed his trecherie, but most of all exclaimed against *Lamilia*: and in her against all enticing Curtizans in these tearmes.

What meant the Poets to inuectiue verse,
To sing Medeas shame, and Scillas pride,
Calipsoes charmes, by which so many dide?
Onely for this, their vices they rehearse,
That curious wits which in this world conuerse,
May shun the dangers and enticing shoes,
Of such false Syrens, those home-breeding foes,
That from their eies their venim do disperse. /
So soone kils not the Basiliske with sight,
The Vipers tooth is not so venomous,
The Adders tung not halfe so dangerous,
As they that beare the shadow of delight,
Who chaine blinde youths in tramels of their haire,
Till wast bring woe, and sorrow hast despaire.

With this he laide his head on his hand, and leant his elbow on the ground sighing out sadly,

> Heu patior telis vulnera facta meis.

On the other side of the hedge sate one that heard his sorrow, who getting ouer, came towardes him, and brake off his passion. When he approached, he saluted *Roberto* in this sort.

Gentleman, quoth hee (for so you seeme), I haue by chaunce heard you discourse some part of your greefe; which appeareth to be more then you will discouer, or I can conceipt. But if you vouchsafe such simple comfort as my abilitie will yeeld, assure[Pg 145] your selfe that I will endeuour to doe the best, that either may procure your profit, or bring you pleasure: the rather, for that I suppose you are a scholler, and pittie it is men of learning should liue in lacke.

Roberto wondring to heare such good words, for that this iron age affoordes few that esteeme of vertue, returned him thankfull gratulations, and (vrged by necessitie) vttered his present griefe, beseeching his aduise how he might be imployed. Why, easily, quoth hee, and greatly to your benefit: for men of my profession get by schollers their whole liuing. What is your profession, sayd *Roberto*? Truely, sir, said he, I am a player. A Player, quoth *Roberto*, I tooke you rather for a gentleman of great liuing, for if by outward habit men shuld be censured, I tell you you would be taken for a substantiall / man. So am I, where I dwell (quoth the player), reputed able at my proper cost to build a Windmill. What though the worlde once went hard with mee, when I was faine to carrie my playing Fardle a footebacke; *Tempora mutantur*, I know you know the meaning of it better then I, but I thus conster it; it is otherwise now; for my very share in playing apparrell will not be solde for two hundred pounds. Truely (said *Roberto*) it is strange, that you should so prosper in that vaine practise, for that it seemes to me your voyce is nothing gracious. Nay then, said the player, I mislike your iudgement: why, I am as[Pg 146] famous for Delphrigus, and the king of Fairies, as euer was any of my time. The twelue labors of *Hercules* haue I terribly thundred on the stage, and placed three scenes of the deuill on the highway to heauen. Haue ye so (said *Roberto*)? then I pray you pardon me. Nay, more (quoth the player), I can serue to make a prettie speech, for I was a countrie Author; passing at a morall, for it was I that pende the Moral of mans wit, the Dialogue of Diues, and for seauen yeeres space was absolute interpreter of the puppets. But now my Almanacke is out of date.

The people make no estimation,
Of Morrals teaching education.

Was not this prettie for a plaine rime extempore? if ye will ye shall haue more. Nay it is enough, said *Roberto*, but how meane you to vse mee? Why sir, in making playes, said the other, for which you shall be well paied, if you will take the paines.

Roberto perceiuing no remedie, thought best to respect of his present necessity, to trie his wit, & went with him willingly: who lodged him at the townes end in a house of retaile, where what happened our Poet you shall / heereafter heare. There, by conuersing with bad company, he grew *A malo in peius*, falling from one vice to another, and so hauing found a vaine to finger crownes he grew cranker then *Lucanio*, who by this time began to droope,[Pg 147] being thus dealt withall by *Lamilia*. She hauing bewitched him with her enticing wiles, caused him to consume, in lesse then two yeares, that infinite treasure gathered by his father with so many a poore mans curse. His lands sold, his iewels pawnd, his money wasted, he was casseerd by *Lamilia* that had coosened him of all. Then walked he like one of duke *Humfreys* Squires, in a threedbare cloake, his hose drawne out with his heeles, his shooes vnseamed, lest his feete should sweate with heate: now (as witlesse as he was) hee remembred his fathers words, his kindnes to his brother, his carelesnesse of himselfe. In this sorrow hee sate downe on pennilesse bench; where, when *Opus* and *Vsus* told him by the chimes in his stomacke it was time to fall vnto meate, he was faine with the *Camelion* to feed vpon the aire, & make patience his best repast.

While he was at his feast, *Lamilia* came flaunting by, garnished with the iewels whereof she beguiled him: which sight serued to close his stomacke after his cold cheere. *Roberto* hearing of his brothers beggerie, albeit he had little remorse of his miserable state, yet did he seeke him out, to vse him as a propertie, whereby *Lucanio* was somewhat prouided for. But being of simple nature, hee serued but for a blocke to whet *Robertoes* wit on; which the poore foole perceiuing, he forsooke all other hopes of life, and fell to be a notorious Pandar: in which detested[Pg 148] course hee continued till death. But *Roberto*, now famozed for an Arch-plaimaking-poet, his purse like the sea somtime sweld, anon like the same sea / fell to a low ebbe; yet seldom he wanted, his labors were so well esteemed. Marry this rule he kept, what euer he fingerd aforehand was the certaine meanes to vnbinde a bargaine, and being asked why he so sleightly dealt with them that did him good? It becomes me, sa[i]th hee, to be contrarie to the worlde, for commonly when vulgar men receiue earnest, they doe performe, when I am paid any thing aforehand I breake my promise. He had shift of lodgings, where in euery place his Hostesse writ vp the wofull remembrance of him, his laundresse, and his boy; for they were euer his in houshold, beside retainers in sundry other places. His companie were lightly the lewdest persons in the land, apt for pilferie, periurie, forgerie, or any villanie. Of these hee knew the casts to cog at Cards, coosin at Dice: by these he learned the legerdemaines of nips, foysters, conni-catchers, crosbyters, lifts, high Lawyers, and all the rabble of that vncleane generation of vipers: and pithily could he paint out their whole courses of craft: So cunning he was in all crafts, as nothing rested in him almost but craftinesse. How often the Gentlewoman his wife laboured vainely to recall him, is lamentable to note: but as one giuen ouer to all lewdnes, he communicated her sorrowful lines among his loose[Pg 149] truls, that iested at her bootelesse laments. If he could any way get credite on scores, he would then brag his creditors carried stones, comparing euerie round circle to a groning

O, procured by a painful burden. The shamefull ende of sundry his consorts, deseruedly punished for their amisse, wrought no compunction in his heart: of which one, brother to a Brothell he kept, was trust vnder a tree as round as a Ball.

To some of his swearing companions thus it happened /: A crue of them sitting in a Tauerne carowsing, it fortuned an honest Gentleman, and his friend, to enter their roome: some of them being acquainted with him, in their domineering drunken vaine, would haue no nay, but downe he must needes sitte with them; beeing placed, no remedie there was, but he must needes keep euen compasse with their vnseemely carrowsing. Which he refusing, they fell from high wordes to sound strokes, so that with much adoe the Gentleman saued his owne, and shifted from their company. Being gone, one of these tiplers forsooth lackt a gold Ring, the other sware they see the Gentleman take it from his hande. Upon this the Gentleman was indited before a Judge: these honest men are deposed: whose wisedome weighing the time of the braule, gaue light to the Iury what power wine-washing poyson had: they, according vnto conscience, found the Gentleman not guiltie, and God released by that verdict the innocent.

[Pg 150]

With his accusers thus it fared: one of them for murther was worthily executed: the other neuer since prospered: the third, sitting not long after upon a lustie horse, the beast suddenly died vnder him: God amend the man.

Roberto euery day acquainted with these examples, was notwithstanding nothing bettered, but rather hardened in wickednesse. At last was that place iustified, God warneth men by dreams and visions in the night, and by knowne examples in the day, but if he returne not, hee comes vpon him with iudgement that shall bee felt. For now when the number of deceites caused *Roberto* bee hatefull almost to all men, his immeasurable drinking had made him the perfect Image of the dropsie, and the loathsome scourge of Lust, tyrannized in his loues: / liuing in extreame pouerty, and hauing nothing to pay but chalke, which now his Host accepted not for currant, this miserable man lay comfortlessely languishing, hauing but one groat left (the iust proportiō of his fathers Legacie) which looking on, he cried: O now it is too late, too late to buy witte with thee: and therefore will I see if I can sell to carelesse youth what I negligently forgot to buy.

Heere (Gentlemen) breake I off *Robertos* speech; whose life in most parts agreeing with mine, found one selfe punishment as I haue doone. Heereafter suppose me the said *Roberto*, and I will goe on with[Pg 151] that hee promised: *Greene* will send you now his groatsworth of wit, that neuer shewed a mitesworth in his life: and though no man now be by to doe me good, yet, ere I die, I will by my repentance indeuor to doe all men good.

Deceiuing world, that with alluring toyes,
Hast made my life the subiect of thy scorne:
And scornest now to lend thy fading ioyes,
To lengthen my life, whom friends haue left forlorne.
How well are they that die ere they be borne,
And neuer see thy sleights, which few men shun,
Till vnawares they helplesse are vndon.

Oft haue I sung of loue, and of his fire,
But now I finde that Poet was aduizde;
Which made full feasts increasers of desire,
And prooues weake loue was with the poore despizde.
For when the life with foode is not suffizde,
What thoughts of loue, what motion of delight;
What pleasance can proceede from such a wight?

Witnesse my want the murderer of my wit,
My rauisht sense of woonted furie reft;

Wants such conceit, as should in Poims sit,
Set downe the sorrow wherein I am left:
But therefore haue high heauens their gifts bereft:
Because so long they lent them me to vse,
And I so long their bountie did abuse.

O that a yeare were graunted me to liue,
And for that yeare my former wits restorde:
What rules of life, what counsell would I giue?
How should my sinne with sorrow then deplore?
[Pg 152] But I must die of euery man abhorde.
Time loosely spent will not againe be woonne,
My time is loosely spent, and I vndone.

O horrenda fames, how terrible are thy assaultes? but *Vermis conscientiæ*, more wounding are thy stings. Ah Gentlemen, that liue to reade my broken and confused lines, looke not I should (as I was woont) delight you with vain fantasies, but gather my follies altogether, and as you would deale with so many parricides, cast them into the fire: call them *Telegones*, for now they kill their father, and euerie lewd line in them written is a deep piercing wound to my heart; euery idle houre spent by any in reading them, brings a million of sorrowes to my soule. O that the teares of a miserable man (for neuer any man was yet more miserable) might wash their memorie out with my death; and that those works with me together might be interd. But sith they cannot, let this my last worke witnes against them with me, how I detest them. Blacke is the remembrance of my blacke works, blacker then night, blacker / then death, blacker then hell.

Learne wit by my repentance (Gentlemen), and let these fewe rules following be regarded in your liues.

1. First in all your actions set God before your eies; for the feare of the Lord is the beginning of wisedome: Let his word be a lanterne

to your feete,[Pg 153] and a light vnto your paths, then shall you stande as firme rocks, and not be mocked.

2. Beware of looking backe: for God will not be mocked; of him that hath receiued much, much shall be demanded.

3. If thou be single, and canst abstaine, turne thy eies from vanitie, for there is a kinde of women bearing the faces of Angels, but the hearts of Deuils, able to intrap the elect if it were possible.

If thou be m[a]rried, forsake not the wife of thy youth, to follow strange flesh; for whoremongers and adulterers the Lord will iudge. The doore of a Harlot leadeth downe to death, and in her lips there dwels destruction; her face is decked with odors, but shee bringeth a man to a morsell of bread and nakednesse: of which myselfe am instance.

5. If thou be left rich, remember those that want, and so deale, that by thy wilfulnes thy self want not: Let not Tauerners and Victuallers be thy Executors; for they will bring thee to a dishonorable graue.

6. Oppresse no man, for the crie of the wronged ascendeth to the eares of the Lord; neither delight to encrease by Usurie, lest thou loose thy habitation in the euerlasting Tabernacle.

7. Beware of building thy house to thy neighbours hurt; for the stones will crie to the timber, We were laide together in bloud: and those that so erect houses, calling / them by their names, shall lie[Pg 154] in the graue like sheepe, and death shall gnaw vpon their soules.

8. If thou be poore, be also patient, and striue not to grow rich by indirect meanes; for goods so gotten shall vanish away like smoke.

9. If thou be a father, maister, or teacher, ioyne good examples with good counsaile; else little auaile precepts, where life is different.

10. If thou be a sonne or seruant, despise not reproofe; for though correction be bitter at the first, it bringeth pleasure in the end.

Had I regarded the first of these rules, or beene obedient at the last: I had not now, at my last ende, beene left thus desolate. But now, though to my selfe I giue *Consilium post facta*; yet to others they may serue for timely precepts. And therefore (while life giues leaue) will send warning to my olde consorts, which haue liued as loosely as myselfe, albeit weakenesse will scarce suffer me to write, yet to my fellowe Schollers about this Cittie, will I direct these few insuing lines.

To those Gentlemen his Quondam acquaintance,
that spend their wits in making Plaies, R. G.
wisheth a better exercise, and wisdome
to preuent his extremities.

If wofull experience may mooue you (Gentlemen) to beware, or vnheard of wretchednes intreate you[Pg 155] to take heed, I doubt not but you will looke backe with sorrow on your time past, and endeuour with repentance to spend that which is to come. Wonder not (for with thee wil I first begin), thou famous gracer of Tragedians, that *Greene*, who hath said with thee like the foole / in his heart, There is no God, should now giue glorie vnto his greatnesse: for penitrating is his power, his hand lies heauie vpon me, he hath spoken vnto me with a voice of thunder, and I haue felt he is a God that can punish enimies. Why should thy excellent wit, his gift, be so blinded, that thou shouldst giue no glory to the giuer? Is it pestilent Machiuilian pollicie that thou hast studied? O punish follie! What are his rules but meere confused mockeries, able to extirpate in small time the generation of mankinde. For if *Sic volo, sic iubeo*, hold in those that are able to command: and if it be lawfull *Fas & nefas* to doe any thing that is beneficiall, onely Tyrants should possesse the earth, and they striuing to exceede in tyranny, should each to other bee a slaughter man; till the mightiest outliuing all, one stroke were left for Death, that in one age man's life should ende.

The brother of this Diabolicall Atheisme is dead, and in his life had neuer the felicitie he aimed at: but as he began in craft, liued in feare and ended in despaire. *Quam inscrutabilia sunt Dei iudicia?* This murderer of many brethren had his conscience seared like [Pg 156] *Caine*: this betrayer of him that gaue his life for him, inherited the portion of *Iudas*: this Apostata perished as ill as *Iulian*: and wilt thou my friend be his Disciple? Looke vnto me, by him perswaded to that libertie, and thou shalt finde it an infernall bondage. I knowe the least of my demerits merit this miserable death, but wilfull striuing against knowne truth, exceedeth al the terrors of my soule. Defer not (with me) till this last point of extremitie; for little knowest thou how in the end thou shalt be visited.

With thee I ioyne young *Iuuenall*, that byting Satyrist, that lastlie with mee together writ a Comedie. Sweete / boy, might I aduise thee, be aduised, and get not many enemies by bitter words: inueigh against vaine men, for thou canst do it, no man better, no man so wel: thou hast a libertie to prooue all, and none more; for one being spoken to, all are offended, none being blamed no man is iniured. Stop shallow water still running, it will rage, tread on a worme and it will turne: then blame not schollers vexed with sharpe lines, if they reproue thy too much libertie of reproofe.

And thou no lesse deseruing then the other two, in some things rarer, in nothing inferiour; driuen (as my selfe) to extreame shifts, a little haue I to say to thee: and were it not an idolatrous oth, I would sweare by sweet *S. George*, thou art vnworthie better [Pg 157] hap, sith thou dependest on so meane a stay. Base minded men al three of you, if by my miserie ye be not warned: for vnto none of you (like me) sought those burres to cleaue: those Puppits (I meane) that speake from our mouths, those Anticks garnisht in our colours. Is it not strange that I, to whom they al haue beene beholding: is it not like that you, to whome they all haue beene beholding, shall (were ye in that case that I am now) be both at once of them forsaken? Yes, trust them not: for there is an vpstart Crow, beautified with our feathers, that with his *Tygers heart wrapt in a Players hide,* supposes he is as well able to bumbast out a blanke verse as the best of you: and being an absolute *Iohannes fac totum*, is in his owne conceit the onely Shake-scene in a countrie. O that I might intreate your rare wits to be imployed in more profitable courses: & let those Apes imitate your past excellence, and neuer more acquaint them with your admired inuentions. I know the best husband of you all will neuer proue an Usurer, and the kindest of them / all will neuer prooue a kinde nurse: yet whilst you may, seeke you better Maisters; for it is pittie men of such rare wits, should be subiect to the pleasures of such rude groomes.

In this I might insert two more, that both haue writ against these buckram Gentlemen: but let their owne works serue to witnesse against their owne[Pg 158] wickednesse, if they perseuer to mainteine any more such peasants. For other new commers, I leaue them to the mercie of these painted monsters, who (I doubt not) will driue the best minded to despise them: for the rest, it skils not though they make a ieast at them.

But now returne I againe to you [t]hree, knowing my miserie is to you no news: and let me heartily intreate you to bee warned by my harmes. Delight not (as I haue done) in irreligious oaths; for from the blasphemers house a curse shall not depart. Despise drunkennes, which wasteth the wit, and maketh men all equal vnto beasts. Flie lust, as the deathsman of the soule, and defile not the Temple of the holy ghost. Abhorre those Epicures, whose loose life hath made religion lothsome to your eares: and when they sooth you with tearmes of Mastership, remember *Robert Greene*, whome they haue so often flattered, perishes now for want of comfort. Remember gentlemen, your liues are like so many lighted Tapers, that are with care deliuered to all of you to maintaine: these with wind-puft wrath may be extinguisht, which drunkennes put out, which negligence let fall: for mans time of itselfe is not so short, but it is more shortened by sin. The fire of my light is now at the last snuffe, and the want of wherwith to sustaine it, there is no substance left for life to feede on. Trust not then (I beseech yee)[Pg 159] to such weake staies: for they /

are as changeable in minde, as in many attires. Well, my hand is tired, and I am forst to leaue where I would begin; for a whole booke cannot containe these wrongs, which I am forst to knit vp in some few lines of words.

Desirous that you should liue, though
himselfe be dying,
Robert Greene.

Now to all men I bid farewell in this sort, with this conceited Fable of the olde Comedian *Æsope*.

An Ant and a Grashopper walking together on a greene, the one carelessely skipping, the other carefully prying what winters prouision was scattered in the way: the Grashopper scorning (as wantons wil) this needelesse thrift (as he tearmed it) reprooued him thus:

The greedie miser thirsteth still for gaine;
His thrift is theft, his weale works others woe:
That foole is fond which will in caues remaine,
When mongst faire sweetes he may at pleasure goe.

To this the Ant perceiuing the Grashoppers meaning, quickly replied:

The thriftie husband spares what vnthrifts spends,
His thrift no theft, for dangers to prouide:
Trust to thy selfe, small hope in want yeeld friendes,
A caue is better than the desarts wide.

[Pg 160]

In short time these two parted, the one to his pleasure / the other to his labour. Anon Haruest grewe on, and reft from the Grashopper his woonted moysture. Then weakely skips he to the medows brinks:

where till fell winter he abode. But stormes continually powring, hee went for succour to the Ant his olde acquaintance, to whome he had scarce discouered his estate, but the little worme made this replie.

Pack hence (quoth he) thou idle lazie worme,
My house doth harbour no vnthriftie mates:
Thou scornedst to toile, and now thou feelst the storme,
And starust for foode while I am fed with cates.
Vse no intreats, I will relentlesse rest,
For toyling labour hates an idle guest.

The Grashopper, foodlesse, helpelesse, and strengthlesse, got into the next brooke, and in the yeelding sand digde himselfe a pit: by which likewise he ingraued this Epitaph.

When Springs greene prime arrayd me with delight,
And euery power with youthfull vigor fild,
Gaue strength to worke what euer fancie wild:
I neuer feard the force of winters spight.

When first I saw the sunne the day begin,
And drie the mornings teares from hearbs and grasse;
I little thought his chearefull light would passe,
Till vgly night with darknes enterd in.
And then day lost I mournd, spring past I waild,
But neither teares for this or that auaild.

Then too too late I praisd the Emmets paine, /
That sought in spring a harbour gainst the heate:
And in the haruest gathered winters meate,
Perceiuing famine, frosts, and stormie raine.

My wretched end may warne Greene springing youth,
To vse delights as toyes that will deceiue,
And scorne the world before the world them leaue:

For all worlds trust, is ruine without ruth.
Then blest are they that like the toyling Ant,
Prouide in time gainst winters wofull want.

With this the grashopper yeelding to the weathers extremit[ie], died comfortlesse without remedie. Like him myselfe: like me, shall al that trust to friends or times inconstancie. Now faint of my last infirmitie, beseeching them that shal burie my bodie, to publish this last farewell, written with my wretched hand.

Fælicem fuisse infaustum.

A letter written to his wife, found with this booke after his death.

The remembrance of many wrongs offered thee, and thy vnreprooued virtues, adde greater sorrow to my miserable state then I can vtter or thou conceiue. Neither is it lessened by consideration[Pg 162] of thy absence (though shame would let me hardly beholde thy face) but exceedingly aggrauated, for that I cannot (as I ought) to thy owne selfe reconcile my selfe, that thou mightest witnesse my inward woe at this instant, that haue made thee a wofull wife for so long a time. But equal heauen hath denied that comfort, giuing at my last neede / like succour as I haue sought all my life: being in this extremitie as voide of helpe as thou hast beene of hope. Reason would, that after so long waste, I should not send thee a childe to bring thee greater charge; but consider he is the fruit of thy wombe, in whose face regard not the fathers faults so much as thy owne perfections. He is yet Greene, and may grow straight, if he be carefully tended: otherwise apt enough (I feare me) to follow his fathers folly. That I haue offended thee highly I knowe; that thou canst forget my iniuries I hardly beleeue: yet perswade I my selfe if thou saw my wretched state thou couldest not but lament it: nay, certainely I knowe thou wouldest. Al my wrongs muster themselues about me, euery euill at once plagues me. For my contempt of God,

I am contemned of men: for my swearing and forswearing, no man will beleeue me: for my gluttony, I suffer hunger: for my drunkennesse, thirst: for my adulterie, vlcerous sores. Thus God hath cast me downe, that I might be humbled: and punished me for example of others sinne: and [Pg 163] although he suffers me in this world to perish without succour, yet trust I in the world to come to finde mercie, by the merits of my Sauiour, to whome I commend this, and commit my soule.

Thy repentant husband for his disloyaltie.

Robert Greene.

Fœlicem fuisse infaustum.

[Pg 164]

FINIS

V., VI.—GABRIEL HARVEY AND THOMAS NASH

(*Characters of Gabriel Harvey and accounts of his quarrel with the Marlowe group, and Nash in particular, will be found in all histories of Elizabethan literature, and also elsewhere. The war of pamphlets between Harvey and Nash was a very furious word-battle, and its two chief monuments,* Pierce's Supererogation *and* Have with you to Saffron Walden, *are as choice examples of scurrility as can easily be found. But both are very long, and as I have set my heart on giving whole pamphlets, I have preferred Harvey's* Precursor *and Nash's* Prognostication. *The former is a sort of pilot engine to* Pierce's Supererogation, *published first before and then with the longer piece, and for all its brevity intensely characteristic of Harvey—the incarnation of the donnishness of his time, and also of a certain side of the Elizabethan man of letters generally. The latter, though evidently composed in direct imitation of Rabelais, of whom Nash was certainly a reader, was indirectly an attack on the Harveys, one of whom, Gabriel's brother Richard, was a great astrologer.*)

Pierces Supererogation

OR

A NEW PRAYSE OF THE
OLD ASSE. *A Preparatiue to certaine larger Discourses, intituled* NASHES S. FAME.

Gabriell Harueypan>.

Il vostro Malignare Non Giova Nvlla.

LONDON
Imprinted by Iohn Wolfe.
1593

[Pg 166]

To my very gentle and liberall frendes, M. Barnabe Barnes, M. Iohn Thorius, M. Antony Chewt, and euery fauorable Reader.

Louing M. Barnabe, M. Iohn, and M. Antony (for the rest of my partiall Cōmenders must pardon me, till the Print be better acquainted with their names), I haue lately receiued your thrise-curteous Letters, with the Ouerplus of your thrise-sweet Sonets annexed: the liberallest giftes, I beleeue, that euer you bestowed vpon so slight occasion, and the very prodigallest fruites of your floorishing wittes. Whose onely default is, not your, but my default, that the matter is nothing correspondent to the manner; and miselfe must either grosely forget miselfe, or franckly acknowledge mi simple selfe an vnworthy subiect of so worthy commendations. Which I cannot read without blushing, repeate without shame, or remember without griefe, that I come so exceeding-short in so excessiue great accountes; the summes of your rich largesse, not of my poore desert; and percase deuised to aduertise me what I should be, or to signifie what you wish [me][Pg 167] to be; not to declare what I am, or to insinuate what I may be. Eloquence, and Curtesie were euer bountifull in the amplifying veine: and it hath bene reputed a frendly Pollicy, to encourage their louing acquaintance to labour the attainement of those perfections, which they blason in them, as already atcheiued. Either some such intention you haue, by / way of Stratageme, to awaken my negligence, or enkindle my confidence; or you are disposed by way of Ciuility, to make me vnreasonably beholding vnto you for your extreme affection. Which I must either leaue vnrequited; or recompense affection with affection, & recommende me vnto you with your owne Stratageme, fitter to animate fresher spirites, or to whet finer edges. Little other vse can I, or the world reape of those great-great commendations, wherewith you, and diuers other Orient wittes haue newly surcharged me, by tendring so many kinde Apologies in my behalfe, and presenting so many sharpe inuectiues against my aduersaries: vnlesse also you purposed to make me notably ashamed of my cōfessed insufficiency, guilty of so manifold imperfectiōs, in respect of the least semblance of those imputed singularities. Whatsoeuer your intendment in an ouerflowing affection was, I am none of those, that greedily surfet of selfe-conceit, or sottishly hugge their owne babyes. *Narcissus* was a fayre boy, but a boy: *Suffenus* a noble braggard, but a braggard: *Nestor* a sweet-tongued old-man, but an Old-man: and *Tully* (whom I honour in his vertues, and excuse in his ouersightes) an eloquent Selfe-loouer, but a Selfe-loouer. He that thought to make himselfe famous with his ouerweening and brauing *Il'e, Il'e, Il'e*, might perhaps nourrish an aspiring imagination to imitate his *Ego, Ego, Ego*, so gloriously reiterated in his gallant Orations. Some smirking minions are fine fellowes in their owne heades, and some cranke Princockes iolly men in their owne humours: as desperate in resolution, as the dowtiest ranke of Errant knightes; and as coye in phantasie, as the nicest sort of simpring damosels, that in their owne glasses find no creature so bewtifull, or amiable, as their delitious selues. I haue beheld, / & who hath not seene some lofty conceites, towring very high, & coying themselues sweetly on their owne amounting winges, young feathers of old Icarus? The gay Peacocke is woondrously inamored vpon the glittering fanne of his owne gorgious taile, and weeneth himselfe worthy to be crowned the Prince of byrdes, and to be enthronished in the chaire of supreme excellency. Would Christ, the greene Popiniay, with his newfangled iestes, as new as Newgate, were not asmuch to say, as his owne Idol. Queint wittes must haue a Priuiledge to prank-vp their dainty limmes, & to fawne vpon their owne tricksie deuises. But they that vnpartially know themselues, seuerely examine their owne abilities; vprightly counterpoise defectes with sufficiencies; frankly confesse the greatest part of their knowledge to be the least part of their ignorance; aduisedly weigh the difficulties of the painfull and toylesome way, the hard maintenance of credit easely gotten, the impossible satisfaction of vnsatisfiable expectation, the vncertaine ficklenesse of priuate Phantasie, & the certaine brittlenesse of publique Fame; are not lightly bewitched with a fonde doting vpon their owne plumes. And they that deepely consider vpon the weakenesse of inward frailty, the casualtie of outward fortune, the detraction of Enuie, the virulency of Malice, the counter-pollicy of Ambition, and a hundred-hundred empeachments of growing reputation: that aswell diuinely, as philosophically haue learned to looue the gentlenesse of Humanity, to embrace the mildnesse of Modestie, to kisse the meekenesse of Humilitie, to loath the odiousnesse of Pride, to assuage the egreness of Spite, to preuent the vengeance of Hatred, to reape the sweet fruites of Temperance, to tread the smooth Path of Securitie, to take the firme course of Assuraunce, / and to enioy the felicitie of Contentment: that iudiciously haue framed themselues to carry Mindes, like their Bodies, and Fortunes, as apperteineth vnto them, that would be loth to ouerreach in presumptuous conceit: they I say, and all they that would rather vnderly the reproche of obscuritie, then ouercharge their mediocritie with an illusiue opinion of extraordinary furni[Pg 170]ture, and I wott not what imaginarie complementes: are readier, and a thousand times readier, to returne the greatest Prayses, where they are debt, then to accept the meanest, where they are almes. And I could nominate some, that in effect make the same reckoning of Letters, Sonets, Orations, or other writinges commendatory, that they do of meate without nourishment, of hearbes without vertue, of plants without fruite; of a lampe without oyle, a linke without light, or a fier without heate. Onely some of vs are not so deuoide of good manner, but we conceiue what belongeth to ciuill duty, and will euer be prest to interteine Curtesie with curtesie, & to requite any frendship with frendship: vnfainedly desirous, rather to recompense in deedes, then to glose, or paint in wordes. You may easely persuade me to publish, that was long sithence finished in writing, and is now almost dispatched in Print: (the amendes must be addressed in some other more materiall Treatise, or more formal

Discourse: and haply *Nashes S. Fame* may supply some defectes of Pierces Supererogation:) but to suffer your thrise-affectionate Letters and Sonets, or rather your thrise lauish beneuolences to be published, which so farre surmount not onely the mediocrity of my present endeuour, but euen the possibility of any my future emproouement; I could not be persuaded by any eloquence, or importunacy in the world, were I not as monstrously / reuiled by some[Pg 171] other without reason, as I am excessively extolled by you without cause. In which case he may seeme to a discreet enemy excusable, to an indifferent frend iustifiable, that is not transported with his owne passion, but relyeth on the iudgement of the learnedest, and referreth himselfe to the Practise of the wisest. In the one, esteeming *Plutarch* or *Homer* as an hundred Autors: in the other, valuing *Cato*, or *Scipio*, as a thousand Examples. I neuer read, or heard of any respectiue, or considerate person, vnder the degree of those that might reuenge at pleasure, contemne with autority, assecure themselues from common obloquy, or commande publique reputation (mighty men may finde it a Pollicy, to take a singular, or extraordinary course), so carelesse of his owne credit, so recklesse of the present time, so senselesse of the posterity, so negligent in occurents of consequence, so dissolute in his proceedings, so prodigall of his name, so deuoide of all regarde, so bereft of common sense, so vilely base, or so hugely hawtie of minde; that in case of infamous imputation, or vnworthy reproch, notoriously scattered-abroad, thought it not requisite, or rather necessary, to stand vpon his owne defence according to Equity, and euen to labour his owne commendation according to the presented occasion. Discourses yeeld plenty of Reasons: and Histories affourde store of Examples. It is no vain-glory to permit with consideration, that abused Modesty hath affected with discretion. It is[Pg 172] vanity to controwle, that true honour hath practised: and folly to condemne, that right wisedome hath allowed. If any dislike Immodesty indeede, despise vanity indeede, reprooue Arrogancy indeede, or loath Vainglory indeede; I am as forward with Tongue and Hart as the foremost of the forwardest: and were / my pen answerable, perhaps at occasion it should not greatly lagge behinde. To accomplish, or aduaunce any vertuous purpose (sith it is now enforced to be sturring), it might easely be entreated, euen to the vttermost extent of that little-little Possibility, wherewith it hath pleased the Greatest to endowe it. Howbeit Curtesie is as ready to ouerloade with prayse as Malice eger to ouerthrow with reproch. Both ouershoote, as the manner is; but malice is the Diuell. For my poore part, I hope the One shall do me as little harme as fayre weather in my iorney: I am suer, the other hath done me more good, then was intended, and shall neuer puddle or annoy the course of the cleere running water. Albeit I haue studied much, and learned little: yet I haue learned to gleane some handfulls of corne out-of the rankest cockle: to make choice of the most fragrant flowers of *Humanitie*, the most vertuous hearbes of *Philosophie*, the most soueraine fruites of *Gouernment*, and the most heauenly manna of *Diuinitie*: to be acquainted with the fayrest, prouided for the fowlest, delighted with the temperatest, pleased with the meanest, and contented with all [Pg 173] *weather*. Greater men may professe, and can atchieue greater matters: I thanke God I know the lēgth, that is, the shortnes of mine owne foote. If it be any mans pleasure to extenuate my sufficiēcy in other knowledge, or practise, to empeach my ability in wordes, or deedes, to debase my fortune, to abridge my commendations, or to annihilate my fame, he shall finde a cold aduersary of him that hath layed hoat passions awatering, and might easely be induced to be the Inuectiue of his owne Non-proficiency. Onely he craueth leaue to estimate his credit, and to value his honesty, as behooueth euery man, that regardeth any good: and if withall it be his / vnfained request, that Order should repeale disorder; moderation restraine licentiousnesse; discretion abandon vanity; mildnesse assuage choller; meeknesse alay arrogancy; consideration reclaime rashnesse; indifferency attemper passion; Curtesie mitigate, Charity appease, & Vnity attone debate: pardon him. Or, in case nothing will preuaile with fury but fury, and nothing can winne desired amity but pretended hostility, that must driue-out one naile with another, & beat-away one wedge with another, according to the Latin Prouerbe: Pardon him also, that in the resolution of a good minde, will commaund, what he cannot entreat; and extort, what he cannot persuade. That little may be done with no great adoo: and, seeing it may as surely, as easely be done, I am humbly to beseech established Wise[Pg 174]dome, to winke at one experiment of aduenturous Folly; neuer before embarked in any such actiō, and euer to eschewe the like with a chary regard, where any other mediation may purchase redresse. I will not vrge what conniuence hath been noted in as disfauorable cases: it is sufficient for me to pleade mine own acquittall. Other prayse he affecteth not, that in a deepe insight into his innermost partes findeth not the highest pitch of his Hope equiualent to the lowest pit of your commendation. And if by a gentle construction, or a fauorous encouragement, he seemeth any thing in others opinion, that is nothing in his owne Censure, the lesser his merite, the greater their mercy; and the barrainer his desert, the frutefuller your liberality. Whose vnmeasurable prayses I am to interpret, not as they may seeme in some bounteous conceit, but as they are in mine owne knowledge; good wordes, but vnfitly applied; frendly beneuolences, but wastfully bestowed; gallant amplifications, but slenderly deser/ued: what but termes of Ciuility, or fauours of Curtesie, or hyperboles of Looue: whose franke allowance I shall not be able to earne with the study of twenty yeares more: in briefe, nothing but partiall witnesses, preiudicate iudgements, idle preambles, and in effect meere wordes. And euen so as I found them, I leaue them. Yet let me not dismisse so extensiue curtesie with an empty hand. Whatsoeuer I am (that am the least little of my thoughtes,[Pg 175] and the greatest contempt of mine owne hart), *Parthenophill* and *Parthenophe* embellished, the *Spanish Counsellour* Inglished, and *Shores Wife* eternised; shall euerlastingly testifie what you are: go forward in maturity, as ye haue begun in pregnancy, and behold *Parthenopoeus* the sonne of the braue Meleager, *Homer* himselfe, and of the swift Atalanta *Calliope* herselfe: be thou, Barnabe, the gallant Poet, like Spencer, or the valiant souldiour, like Baskeruile; and euer remember thy *French seruice* vnder the braue Earl of Essex. Be thou, Iohn, the many-tongued Linguist, like Andrewes, or the curious Intelligencer, like Bodley; and neuer forget *thy Netherlandish traine* vnder Him, that taught the Prince of Nauarre, now the valorous king of Fraunce. Be thou Antony, the flowing

Oratour, like Dooue, or the skilfull Heralde, like Clarentius; and euer remember *thy Portugall voyage* vnder Don Antonio. The beginning of vertuous Proceedings is the one halfe of honorable actions. Be yourselues in hope, and what yourselues desire in effect: and I haue attained some portion of my request. For you cannot wish so exceeding-well vnto me, but I am as ready with tongue, and minde, to wish a great-deale better vnto you, and to reacquite you with a large vsury of most-affectionate prayers, recommending you to the diuine giftes and gratious blessings of Heauen.

May / it please the fauorable Reader, to voutsafe[Pg 176] me the Curtesie of his Patience, vntill he hath thoroughly perused the whole Discourse at his howers of leysure (for such scriblings are hardly worth the vacantest howers): I am not to importune him any farther; but would be glad he might finde the Whole lesse tedious in the end, then some Parts in the beginning, or midst; or, at-least, that one peece might helpe to furnish-out amendes for an other. And so taking my leaue with the kindest Farewell of a most thankfull minde, I desist from wearying him with a tedious Preface, whom I am likely to tire with so many superfluous Discourses. Howbeit might it happely please the sweetest Intercessour to ensweeten the bitterest gall of Spite, and to encalme the roughest tempest of Rage, I could cordially wish that *Nashes S. Fame* might be the Period of my Inuectiues: and *the excellent Gentlewoman*, my patronesse, or rather Championesse in this quarrel, is meeter by nature, and fitter by nurture, to be an enchaunting Angell, with her white quill, then a tormenting Fury with her blacke inke. It remaineth at the election of one, whom God indue with more discretion.

At London: this 16. of July, 1593. The inuiolable frend of his entire frendes, Gabriell Haruey. /

Her owne Prologue, or Demurr.

O Muses, may a wooman poore, and blinde,
A Lyon-draggon, or a Bull-beare binde?

[Pg 177] Ist possible for puling wench to tame
The furibundall Champion of Fame?
He brandisheth the whurlewinde in his mouth,
And thunderbolteth so-confounding shott:
Where such a Bombard-goblin, North, or South,
With drad Pen-powder, and the conquerous pott?
Silly it is, that I can sing, or say:
And shall I venture such a blustrous fray?
Hazard not, panting quill, thy aspen selfe:
Hel'e murther thy conceit, and braine thy braine.
Spare me, ô super domineering Elfe,
And most, *railipotent* for euer raine,
Si Tibi vis ipsi parcere, parce Mihi.

Her Counter-sonnet, or Correction of her owne Preamble.

Scorne frump the meacock Verse that dares not sing,
Drouping, so like a flagging flowre in raine:
Where doth the *Vrany* or *Fury* ring,
That shall enfraight my stomacke with disdaine?
Shall Frend put-vp such braggardous affrontes?
Are milksop Muses such whiteliuer'd Trontes?
Shall Boy the gibbet be of Writers all,
And none hang-vp the gibbet on the wall?
If / dreery hobbling Ryme hart-broken be,
And quake for dread of Danters scarecrow Presse:
Shrew Prose, thy pluckcrow implements addresse,
And pay the hangman pen his double fee.
Be Spite a Sprite, a Termagant, a Bugg:
Truth feares no ruth, and can the Great Diu'll tugg.
——*Ultrix accincta flagello.*

Her old Comedy, newly intituled.

My Prose is resolute, as Beuis sworde:
March rampant beast in formidable hide:
[Pg 178] *Supererogation Squire on cockhorse ride:*
Zeale shapes an aunswer to the blouddiest worde.
If nothing can *the booted Souldiour* tame,
Nor Ryme, nor Prose, nor Honesty, nor Shame,
But *Swash* will still his trompery aduaunce,
Il'e leade the *gagtooth'd fopp* a new-founde daunce.
Deare howers were euer cheape to pidling me:
I knew a glorious, and brauing Knight,
That would be deem'd a truculentall wight:
Of him I scrauld a dowty Comedy.
Sir Bombarduccio was his cruell name:
But *Gnasharduccio* the sole brute of *Fame*.

L'Enuoy.

See, how He brayes, and fumes at me poore lasse,
That must immortalise the killcowe *Asse.* /

To the Right Worshipfvll, his especiall deare frend, M. Gabriell Haruey, Doctour of Lawe.

Sweet M. Doctour Haruey (for I cannot intitule you with an Epithite of lesse value then that which the Grecian and Roman Oratours ascribed to Theophrastus, in respect of so many your excellent labours, garnished with the garland of matchlesse Oratory): if at any time either the most earnest persuasion of a deare frend, and vnusually most deare, and constant, adiured therevnto by the singular vertue of your most prayse-worthy, and vnmatchable wit: or the woonderful admiration of your peerlesse conceit, embraued with so many gorgeous ornamentes of diuine Rhetorique:[Pg 179] or the doubtlesse successive benefit thereof, deuoted to the glory of our English Eloquence, and our vulgar Tuscanisme (if I may so terme it); may worke any plausible or respectiue motions with you to bewtifie, and enrich our age, with those most praise-moouing workes, full of gallantest discourse, and reason, which I vnderstand by some assured intelligence be now glowing vpon the anvile, ready to receiue the right artificiall forme of diuinest workemāship: thē let I beseech you, nay, by all our mutuall frendships I coniure you (loue and admiration of them arming me with the placarde of farther confidence) those, and other your incomparable writings, speedily, or rather pre/sently, shew thēselues in the shining light of the Sunne. That, by this Publication of so rare, & rich Discourses, our English Rauens, the spitefull enemyes to all birdes of more bewtifull wing, and more harmonious note then themselues, may shroude themselues in their nests of basest obscurity, & keepe hospitality with battes, and owles, fit consorts for such vile carions. Good Sir, arise, and confound those Viperous Cryticall monsters, and those prophane Atheistes of our Commonwealth; which endeuour with their mutinous and Serpentine hissing, like geese, not to arme the Senatours and Oratours of Rome, but to daunt, astonish, and, if it were possible, to ouerthrow them. And sithence the very thunder-lightning of your admirable Eloquence is sufficiētly auailable to[Pg 180] strike them with a lame Palsie of tongue (if they be not already smitten with a sencelesse Apoplexy in head, which may easely ensewe such contagious Catharres and Reumes, as I am priuy some of them haue been grieuously disseased withall), misse not, but hitt them seurly home, as they deserue with Supererogation. You haue bene reputed euermore, since first I heard of you in Oxford and elsewhere, to haue bene as much giuen to fauour, commende, and frequent such as were approoued, or toward in learning, witt, kinde behauiour, or any good quality, as may be required in any man of your demerit: an vndoubted signe, how much you loath Inuectiues or any needeles contētions. I would (as many your affectionate frēds would) it had bene your fortune to haue encountred some other Paranymphes, then such as you are now to discipline: most vnwillingly, I perceiue, but most necessarily, & not without especiall consideration, being so manifestly vrged, and grosely prouoked to defend yourselfe. But you haue ere now bene acquainted / with patience perforce: and I hope the most desperate swasher of them will one day learne to shew himself honester or wiser. And thus recommending your sweete endeuours, with your grauer studies, to the highest treasury of heauenly Muses; I right hartely take my leaue with a Sonnet of that Muse, that honoreth the Vrany of du Bartas, and yourselfe: of du Bartas elsewhere; here of him,[Pg 181] whose excellent Pages of the French King, the Scottish King, the braue Monsieur de la Nöe, the aforesayd Lord du Bartas, Sir Philip Sidney, and sundry other worthy personages, deserue immortall commendation. I thanke him very hartely that imparted vnto me those fewe sheetes: and if all be like them, truly all is passing notable, and right singular.

SONNET.

Those learned *Oratours*, Roomes auncient sages,
Persuasions Pith, directours of affection,
The mindes chief counsail, rhetoriques perfection,
The pleasaunt baulms of peace, warres fierce outrages:
Sweet Grecian *Prophets*, whose smooth Muse assuages
The Furies powerfull wrath, poisons infection:
Philosophers (by Causes due connexion,
Match't with th' Effects of Nature) future ages
Embrauing with rich documents of Art: /
The wisest *States-men* of calme Commonweales:
The learned *Generall Councels*, which impart
Diuinest laws, whose wholesome Physique Heales
Both Church, and Layety: All in *one* beholde
Ennobled Arts, as Precious stones in golde.

From my lodging in Holborne: this of June. 1593. Your most affectionate,

Barnabé Barnes.

Hauing perused my former Sonet, if it may please you, Sir, to do asmuch for your deare frends *Parthenophill*, and *Parthenophe*, they shall haue the desired[Pg 182] fruite of their short exercise, and will rest beholding to your curteous acceptance: which they would be glad to reacquite in the loouingest manner they may. And so most affectionatly recommend themselues vnto your good self: whose vnblemished fame they will euermore maintaine with the best bloud of their hartes, tongues, and Pennes. We will not say, how much we long to see the whole Prayses of your two notorious enemyes, the *Asse* and the *Foxe*.

SONET.

Nash, or the confuting Gentleman.

The Muses scorne; the Courtiers laughing-stock;
The Countreys Coxecombe; Printers proper new;
The Citties Leprosie; the Pandars stew;
Vertues disdayne; honesties aduerse rock;
Enuies vile champion; slaunders stumblingblock.
Graund / Oratour of Cunny-catchers crew;
Base broaching tapster of reports vntrue;
Our moderne Viper, and our Countryes mock;
True Valors Cancer-worme, sweet Learnings rust.
Where shall I finde meete colours, and fit wordes,
For such a counterfaict, and worthlesse matter?
Him, whom thou raylest on at thine owne lust,
Sith *Bodine* and sweet *Sidney* did not flatter,
His Inuectiue thee too much grace affordes.

Parthenophil.

[Pg 183]

SONET.

Haruey, *or the sweet Doctour.*

Sidney, sweet Cignet, pride of Thamesis;
Apollos laurell; Mars-his proud prowesse:
Bodine, register of Realmes happinesse,
Which Italyes, and Fraunces wonder is:
Hatcher, with silence whom I may not misse:
Nor *Lewen*, Rhetoriques richest noblesse:
Nor *Wilson*, whose discretion did redresse
Our English Barbarisme: adioyne to this
Diuinest morall *Spencer*: let these speake
By their sweet Letters, which do best vnfould
Harueys deserued praise: since my Muse weake
Cannot relate somuch as hath bene tould
By these *Fornam'd*: then, vaine as it were to bring
New feather to his Fames swift-feathered wing.

Parthenophe.

The Printers Aduertissement to the Gentleman Reader.

CURTEOUS Gentlemen, it seemed good to M. Doctour Haruey, for breuity-sake, and because he liked not ouer-long Preambles, or Postambles, to short discourses, to omit the commendatorie Letters, and Sonnets of M. Thorius, M. Chewt, and diuers other his affectionate frendes of London, and both the Vniuersities. Which neuerthelesse, are reserued to be prefixed, inserted, or annexed, either in his *defensiue Letters*, enlarged with certaine new Epistles of more speciall note; or in his *Discourses of Nashes S. Fame*,[Pg 184] already finished, & presently to be published, as these shall like their interteinement: of whose fauorable & plausible Welcome, diuers learned and fine wittes haue presumed the best. Howbeit finally it was thought not amisse, vpon conference with some his aduised acquaintance, to make choice of some two or three of the reasonablest, and temperatest Sonnets (but for variety, & to auoyde tediousnesse in the entrance, rather to be annexed in the end, then prefixed in the beginning of the present Discourses): one of the foresayd M. Thorius, an other of M. Chewt, and the third of a learned French gentleman, Monsieur Fregeuill Gautius, who hath published some weighty Treatises, aswell Politique as Religious, both in Latin and French; and hath acquainted M. Doctour Haruey with certaine most profitable Mathematicall deuises of his own inuention. The residue is not added by me, but annexed by the Autor himselfe: whom I humbly recommende to your curteous Censure, and so rest from ouertroubling you with my unpolished lines.

[Pg 185]

A Wonderfull

strange and miraculous, Astro-
logicall Prognostication for
this yeer of our Lord God.
1591.

Discouering such wonders to
happen this yeere, as neuer chaunced
since Noes floud.

Wherein if there be found one lye,
the Author will loose his credit
for euer.

By Adam Fouleweather, Student
in Asse-tronomy.

Imprinted at London by *Thomas*
Scarlet.
(1591.)

[Pg 186]

To the Readers health.

SITTING Gentlemen vpon Douer cliffes, to quaint my selfe with the art of Navigation, and knowe the course of the Tides, as the Danske Crowes gather on the Sandes against a storme: so there appeared on the downs such a flock of knaues, that, by Astrological coniectures, I began to gather that this yeere would proue intemperate by an extreme heat in Sōmer, insomuch that the stones in Cheap side should be so hot, that diuers persons should feare to goe from Poules to the Counter in the Poultrye: whereupon I betook me to my Ephimerides, and erecting a figure, haue found such strange accidents to fall out this yeere, Mercury being Lord and predominate in the house of Fortune, that many fooles shall haue full cofers, and wise men walke vp and downe with empty pursses: that if Iupiter were not ioyned with him in a fauourable aspect, the Butchers / of East-cheape should doo little or nothing all Lent but make prickes: seeing therefore the wonders that are like to fall out this present yeere, I haue for the benefit of my Countrymen taken in hand to make[Pg 187] this Prognostication, discoursing breefelye of the Eclipses both of Sunne and Moone, with their dangerous effectes like to followe, which if God preuent not, many poore men are like to fast on Sondaies for want of food, and such as haue no shooes to goe barefoot, if certaine deuout Coblers proue not the more curteous: but yet Astrologie is not so certaine but it may fayle: and therfore diuers Hostesses shall chaulke more this yeere then their Guests wil wipe out: So that I conclude, whatsoeuer is saide by art. *Sapiens dominabitur astris.*

Your freend and Student in Asse-trologie.

Adam Fouleweather. /

Of the Eclipses that shall happen this present yeere, to the great and fearfull terrifying of the beholders.

IF *we may credit* the authenticall censures of Albumazan and Ptolomey, about the motions of celestiall bodies, whose influence dooth exitat and procure continuall mutability in the lower region: we shal finde y^t the Moon this yeere shall be eclipsed, which shall happen in one of ye 12 moneths, & some of the foure / quarters of the yeere, whose pointes as they shall be totallye darkened, so the effectes shall be wondrous and strange. For Cancer being the sole house of the Moone, dooth presage that this[Pg 188] yeere fruits shall be greatly eaten with Catterpillers: as Brokers, Farmers, and Flatterers, which feeding on the sweate of other mens browes, shall greatlye hinder the beautye of the spring, and disparage the growth of all hottest hearbes, vnlesse some northerly winde of Gods vengāce cleere the trees of such Catterpillers, with a hotte plague and the pestilence: but Cancer being a watrie signe and cheefe gouernour of flouds and streams, it foresheweth that Fishmongers if they be not well lookt to, shall goe downe as farre as Graues end in Wherries and forestall the market, to the great preiudice of the poore, that all Lent ground their fare on the benefit of Salte fishe and red herring: besides it signifieth that Brewers shal make hauocke of Theames water, and put more liquour then they were accustomed amongst their Maulte: to the ouerthrowe of certain crased Ale knights, whose morning draughtes of strong Beere is a great staye to their stomacks: a lamentable case if it be not lookt into and preuented by some speedye supplication to the woorshipfull order of ale cunners. / But in this we haue great hope that because the effects cannot surprise the cause, diuers Tapsters shall trust out more then they can get in: and although they fill their Pots but halfe full, yet for want of true dealing die in the Brewers debt.

Thus much for the watry signe of Cancer, and because this Eclipse is little visible in our horison, I[Pg 189] passe it ouer with this prouiso to all seafaring men, to cary more shirts then one with them a ship boord, lest to their great labor they spend many houres in murthering their vermin on the hatches.

The Eclipse of the Sunne.

THE Eclipse of the Sun according to Proclus opinion is like to produce many hot and pestilent infirmities, especiallie amongst Sumners and Petti-foggers, whose faces being combust with many fiery inflamatiues shall shew ye dearth, that by their deuout drinking is like to ensue of Barly, if violent death take not away such cōsuming mault worms: diuers are like to be troubled with such hotte rewmes in their heads, that their haire shall fall off: and such hot agues shall raigne this yeere, with strange feuers and calamaties, that / if the Sunne were not placed in a colde signe, Renish wine would rise to ten pence a quarte before the latter end of August: but diuers good Planets being retrog[r]ade, foretelleth that Lemmans this yeere shalbe plenty, insomuch that many shall vse them to bedward, for the quallifying of their hot and inflamed stomackes. And Mars being placed neere vnto the Sunne sheweth that there shalbe a great death among people: olde women that can liue no longer shall dye for age: and yong men that haue Vsurers to their father, shal this yeer haue[Pg 190] great cause to laugh, for the Deuill hath made a decree, that after they are once in hell, they shall neuer rise againe to trouble their executors: Beside that by all coniecturall argumentes the influence of Mars shall be so violent, that diuers souldiers in partes beyond the seas, shall fall out for want of their paye, and heere in our meridionall clyme, great quarrelles shall be raised between man and man, especially in cases of Law: gentry shall goe check-mate with Iustice, and coyne out countenance ofttimes equitie: the poore sitting on pennylesse benche, shall sell their Coates to striue for a strawe, and Lawyers laugh such fooles to scorne as cannot keep their crownes in their pursses.

Further, there is like to be great falling out amongst / Church men and certaine fond sects of religion like to trouble the commons: selfe conceipters and ouer holy counterfeites that delight in singularitie, shall rise vp and despise authoritie, presuming euen to abuse the higher powers, if Saturne with a frowning influence, did not threaten them with Tibornes consequence. But whereas the Sun is darkned but by digits, and that vpon ye south points, it presageth great miseries to Spain and those Southerly Countries: Friers and Monks shal heat them so this yeer with confessing of Harlots, that their crownes shall wax balde of the one accord, to the great impouerishing of the Spanish Barbers: Surgeons in[Pg 191] Spain shall wax rich, and their Hospitals poore: such a pestilent mortallitie is like to fall amongst those hipocriticall massemongers. The Dukes, Marquesses & Counties shall haue their dublets closed with such Spanish buttons, that they shal neuer proue good quiresters, for the hotte and inflamed rewmes fallen down into their throats: It is further to be feared, that because the Eclipse hapneth in Iulye, there will through the extrem heat grow such abundāce of Fleas, that women shall not goe to bed before twelue a clocke at night, for the great murthers and stratagems they are like to commit vpon those little animalls.

And whereas this Eclipse falleth out at three of the clocke in the afternoone, it foresheweth that manye shall goe soberer into Tauernes then they shall come out: and that he which drinkes hard and lyes cold, shal neuer dye of the sweate, although Gemini combust and retrog[r]ade, sheweth that some shall haue so sore a sweating, that they may sell their haire by the pound to stuffe Tennice balles: but if the Beadelles of Bridewell be carefull this Summer, it may be hoped that Peticote lane may be lesse pestered with ill aires then it was woont: and the houses there so cleere clensed, that honest women may dwell there without any dread of the whip and the carte: and I finde that the altitude of that place and of Shordich are all one eleuated, and 2 degrees,[Pg 192] and vnder the zenith or verticall point of Venus, which presageth that sundry sorts of men and women shall be there resident: some shalbe so short heeld & so quesie stomackt that they shal ly in their beds while noon, by which means they shal grow so ful of grosse humors, that they shalbe troubled with strange timpanies & swellings in their bellies, vncurable for fortye weekes vntill they be helped by the aduice of some skilfull Midwife.

Besides, other of the same sex and faction, / shall learn to cosin young nouices, and fetch in young Gentlemen, to the great ouerthrow of youth, if some sharpe and speedye redresse be not fetcht from the woorshipfull Colledge of the Phisitians in the parrish of S. Brides. But heere by the waye gentle Reader, note that this Eclipse sheweth, that this yeer shall be some strange birthes of Children produced in some monstrous forme, to the greefe of the Parentes, and fearefull spectackle of the beholders: but because the Eclipse chaunseth Southerlye, it is little to be feared that the effectes shall fail in England: yet somewhat it is to bee doubted, that diuers Children shall be borne, that when they come to age shall not knowe their owne Fathers: others shall haue their fingers of [t]he nature of Lyme twigges, to get most parte of their liuing with fiue and a reache: some shall be born with feet like vnto Hares, that they shal run so swift, that they shall neuer tarry with [Pg 193] maister, but trudge from poste to piller, till they take vp beggars bush for their lodging: Others shall haue Noses like Swine, that there shall not be a feast within a myle, but they shall smell it out: But especiallye it is to be doubted, that diuers women this yeere shall bee borne with two tungs, to the terrible greefe of such as shall marry them, vttering / in their furye such rough cast eloquence, that knaue and slaue shalbe but holyday woords to their husbands. And whereas this fearefull Eclipse dooth continue but an houre and a halfe, it signifieth that this yeere womens loue to their husbands shall be very shorte, some so momentarye, that it shall scarce continue from the Church doore to the wedding house: and that Hennes, Capons, Geese, and other pullin shall little haunt poore mens tables, but flye awaye with spittes in their bellies to fatte Churlles houses, that pamper themselues vp with delicates and dainties: although very fewe other effectes are to be prognosticated, yet let me giue this caueat to my Countrymen, as a clause to this wonderfull Eclipse. Let such as haue clothes enow, keep themselues warme from taking of colde: and I would wishe rich men all this winter to sit by a good fire, and hardlye to goe to bed without a Cuppe of Sack, and that so qualified with Suger, that they proue not rewmatick: let them feede daintilye and take ease enough, and no doubt according to the iudgement of Albumazar, [Pg 194] they are like to liue as long as they can, and not to dye one hower before their time.

Thus much for this strange Eclipse of the Sunne.

Of / the second Eclipse of the Moone, which is like to fall out when it chaunseth either before the 31. of December or els not at all, this present yeere. 1591.

The second Eclipse of the Moon shalbe but little seene in England, wherevpon the effectes shall be nothing preiuditiall to our clyme: yet as the bodye of the Moone is neuer obscure in part or in whole, but some dangerous euents doo followe: so I meane to set downe breefely what is to be lookte for in these westerne partes of the worlde.

First therefore it is to bee feared, that the Danes shall this yeere bee greatly giuen to drincke, insomuch that English Beere shall there be woorth fiue pence a stoape, that their Hoffes and tappe houses shall be more frequented then the Parishe Churches, and many shall haue more Spruce Beere in their bellies, then wit in their heads: wherevpon shall / growe Apoplexies and colde palsies in their legges, that they shall diuers times not bee able to stand on their feete. Vpon this shall growe great commoditye to the Potters and Glasse makers, for it is like there shall be a great ouerthrowe of them, if there bee not some act made for drinking in blacke Jackes.[Pg 195] But if the weather prooue seasonable, and the Haruest great, and the Barnes full of Corne: Rye is like to be cheap in Denmarke, and bread to be of a reasonable size, for the releeuing of the poore. Mar[r]y, Fraunce is like to haue a great dearth of honest men, if the king preuaile not against these mutenous Rebelles of the League, and Papists in diuers places to be plentye, if God or the King rout them not out with a sharpe ouerthrow: But this hope we haue against that rascall rabble of those shauelings, that there was found in an olde booke this Prophecie spoken about Jerusalem long since by a Jew: The tree that God hath not planted shall be pulled vp by the roots: some curious Astronomers of late dayes that are more Propheticall than Juditiall, affirme that Martin the kill-hog for his deuout drincking (by the Pope canonized a Saint) shall rise againe in the apparell of a Minister, and tickle some of the baser sorte with such lusty humors in their braines, that / diuers selfe conceited fooles shal become his disciples, and grounding their witlesse opinion on an heriticall foundation, shall seeke to ruinate authoritie, and peruert all good orders established in the Church, to the great preiudice of vnity and religion, tituling thēselues by the names of Martinistes, as the Donatists grew from Donates: were it not that the Moone being in Taurus, which gouernes the neck and throat, shewes that the Squinancie shall raigne amongst them, and [Pg 196] diuers for want of breath dye of the strangling. Now for that Capricornus is a signe wherein Luna is often resident, it prognosticateth a great death amongst hornde beasts. The Butchers shall commit wilfull murther vpon Sheepe and Oxen, and diuers Keepers kill store of Buckes, and reserue no other fees to their selues but the hornes, insomuche that if the Person of Horne-Church in Essex take not heede, there maye hap to prooue this yeere some Cuckoldes in his Parrish.

But there is like to bee concluded by an act set downe in Grauesende Barge, that hee that wypes his Nose and hath it not, shall forfeite his whole face, and that all such as are iealous ouer their wiues without cause, are worthie to bee punisht with / the horne plague for their labour. And whereas this Eclipse is farre from the signe Pisces, it shewes that there shall bee much stinking fish this yere at Billings gate, and that Quinborowe oyster boates shall ofte times carrie knaues as wel as honest men: but let the Fish-wiues take heed, for if most of them proue not scoldes, yet because Pisces is a signe that gouernes the feete, they shall weare out more shooes in Lent then in anie two months beside through the whole yeere, and get their liuing by walking and crying, because they slaundered Ram alley with such a tragical infamie. The rest I conceale as friuolous, and little necessarie to be touched in this Prognostication.

[Pg 197]

A declaration of the generall disposition of sundrie conceited qualities incident vnto mens mindes & natures throughout these foure quarters of the yere, by the merrie influence of the Planets, with some other tragicall euents and obseruations worthie the noting, contayned vnder each seperated reuolution.

And first of the inclination of the Winter quarter.

Winter / the first Astronomicall quarter of the yeare, according to my vsuall account, whatsoever Ptolomie says, beginneth sooner with poore men than with rich, graunted so by the malignant influence of Saturne, whose constellation is that suche as haue no money nor credit, shall want coles & woode, and be faine to stand and starue for colde, while olde pennifathers sit and wast them selues by the fire. The winter beginning at that instant when the Sunne makes his entraunce into the first degree of Capricornus, that Hiemall solstitiall signe shewes that by naturall inclination this quarter is generally fleugmatike, and that all shall be of suche great authoritie, that the Bakers Basket shall giue the wall vnto the Brewers Barrell, and a halfe pennye drie doe homage vnto a halfe pennye wet. The weather and season being so colde that diuerse for feare of the frost shall sit all daye at Tables and Cardes, while their poore wiues and families fast at home for their follies. And in respect that I finde three of the seauen[Pg 198] Planetes to be in waterie signes as Juppiter, Mars, and the Moone, it signifieth that diuerse persons, both men and women, for want of wine or strong drinke shall goe to bedde sober against their willes. That Sea-faring men shall haue ill lucke if / either their shippes hit agaynst rockes or sticke in the sandes, that there shall bee such great hoarie frostes, that men and women shall creepe to bedde together, and some of them lie so long till they bee fetchte out with a Bason. Heere Saturne retrograde in Gemini, shewes that there shall this Winter fall such great fogs and mists, that diuerse riche men shall loose their purses by the high waie side, and poore men be so weather beaten by the crafte of vsurers, that they shall begge their bread by the extremitie of such extortion: but Mercurie and Venus beeing congregated in Sagitarie, prognosticateth that for want of faire weather, such as haue but one shirt shall go woolward till that be a washing, and that water-men that want fares shall sit and blowe their fingers till theyr fellowes row betwixte the Old Swanne and Westminister. And by reason that Mars that malignant Planet, hath nothing to doe in that Hiemall reuolution, souldiers this Winter for the most parte, shall lie still in garrisons, and shall not be troubled with more monie than is necessarie. Beeing also greatly to bee feared, that through the extreame colde diuerse poore men shall die at riche mennes doores:[Pg 199] pittie shall bee exiled, good woorkes trust ouer the sea with Jacke / a lent and Hospitalitie banisht as a signe of popish religion: and were it not that some moist shoures shal moderate the hardnes of the frost, Charitie should for want of house roome lie and freeze to death in the streets: diuerse great stormes are this yere to be feared, especially in houses where the wiues weare the breeches, with such lowde windes, that the women shall scolde their husbandes quight out of doores, wherevpon is like to fall great haile-stones as bigge as ioynd stooles, that some shall haue their heads broken: and all through the froward disposition of Venus. But Mars comes in and playes the man, who beeing placed in Gemini, that gouerns armes and shoulders, presageth that sundrie tall fellowes shall take heart at grasse, who armed with good cudgels, shall so lambeake these stubborne huswiues, that the wind shall turne into another quarter, and so the weather waxe more calme and quiet. Such greate floudes are like to insue, through this Hiemall distemperature, that diuerse men shall be drowned on drie hilles, and fishe if they could not swimme, were vtterly like to perish. Eeles are like to bee deere if there bee few or none taken, and plentie of poutes to bee had in all places, especiallie in those coastes and Countries where weomen haue / not their owne willes. Nowe Gentle Reader in respect of diuerse particular circumstances,[Pg 200] drawne from the daily motions, progressions, stations, retrogradations, aspects, and other appointmentes of fixed and wandring stars, I am induced to set downe that such as haue no fire, shall feele most cold, and that wierdrawers, if they plye not their worke, shall feele no great heate, that they in Russia shall suffer more preiudice by the sharpenesse of Winter than the Spaniards: and yet one thing is to bee hoped for at the handes of Mercurie, that this winter mony shall haue a fall, for

Philip and Mary shillings that heretofore went for 12d. shall now passe from man to man for 6d. a peece.

The distemperance of this quarter, is like to breede many sicknesses and sundrie diseases as well in young as in old, proceeding either of corrupt and vicious bloud or of superabundance of crude and raw fleugmatike humors. As Cephala[l]gies or paines in the head, which shall make men dizzy that some shal stagger & stumble vp & downe the streetes till they haue stolne a nappe to quiet their braines. Ach in the shoulders shal raine amongest diuerse women that haue shrewes to their husbands, and diuerse drunken men shall be pestured with surfets. Maidens this winter shall haue strange stitches & gripings / of the collicke, which diseases proceed by too much lying vpright: and men shall be troubled with such paine in the eies, that they shall not know their owne wiues from other women, with coughs, rumes, and itchings, which I omit.

[Pg 201]

Of the Spring time.

Winter being finished with the last grade of the watry signe Pisces, at the Suns ioyful progresse into the first degree of Aries. The second quarter of our vsuall yere commonly called the spring cōmeth next, which beginneth when grasse begins to sproute, & trees to bud. But to treat of this present season, forasmuch as I find the planets to be contradictorily disposed, in signs & mansiōs of diuerse & repugnant qualities, I gather that this spring will be very il for schollers, for they shal studie much and gain litle, they shal haue more wit in their heads then money in their purses, dunces shal proue more welthie then diuers doctors, insomuch that sundrie vnlettered fooles should creep into the ministerie, if the prouident care of good Bishops did not preuent thē. And by the opinion of Proclus, women are like to grow wilful, & so variable, that they shall laugh & weepe, and all with a winde: Butchers shal sell / their meate as deare as they can, and if they be not carefull, horne beastes shall bee hurtfull vnto them, and some shall bee so wedded to swines flesh, that they shall neuer be without a sowe in their house as long as they liue. This spring, or vernall resolution being naturally hot and moist, is like to be verie forwarde for sprouting fieldes and blooming trees, and because Saturne is in his proper mansion, olde[Pg 202] men are like to bee froward, and craftie knaues shall neede no Brokers, vsurie shalbe called good husbandrie, and men shalbe counted honest by their wealth, not by their vertues. And because Aquarius has somthing to do wt this quarter, it is to be doubted that diuers springs of water will rise vp in vintners sellers, to the great weakning of their Gascon wine, & the vtter ruine of the ancient order of the redde noses. March Beere shalbe more esteemed than small Ale.

Out of the old stocke of heresie, this spring it is to be feared, will bloome new scismaticall opinions and strange sects, as Brownists, Barowists, & such balductum deuises, to the great hinderance of the vnitie of the Church, & confusion of the true faith, if the learned doctor sir T. Tiburne be not taskte to confute such vpstart companions, with his plain & dunstable philosophie. Cancer is bu/sie in this springtide, and therefore it is like that florishing bloomes of yong gentlemens youth, shalbe greatly anoide with caterpillers, who shall intangle them in such statutes & recognances, that they shall crie out against brokers, as Jeremy did against false prophets. Besides, thogh this last winter nipt vp diuers masterles men & cut purses, yet this spring is like to afford one euery tearme this ten yere in Westminster hall: Barbers if they haue no worke are like to grow poore, and for that Mercury is[Pg 203] cōbust and many quarelles like to growe amongst men, lawiers shall proue rich & weare side gowns and large consciences, hauing theyr mouths open to call for fees, and theyr purses shut when they shoulde bestowe almes. But take heed O you generation of wicked Ostlers, that steale haie in the night from gentlemens horses, and rub their teth with tallow, that they may eate little when they stand at liuery, this I prognosticate against you, that this spring, which so euer of you dies, shall leaue a knaues carcasse in the graue behind him, and that they which liue shall hop a harlot in his clothes all the yere after. But aboue all let me not hide this secret from my countrymen, that Jupiter being in aspect with Luna, discouereth that diuers men shal drinke more thē they bleed, & / Tailers shall steale nothing but what is brought vnto them, that poulters shall bee pestered with rotten egs, & Butchers dogs make libels against Lent, that affoordes no foode but herring cobs for their diet.

Diseases incident to this quarter, as by Astrologicall & philosophicall coniectures I can gather, are these following: Prentises that haue ben fore beaten, shall be troubled with ach in their armes, and it shall be ill for such as haue fore eies, to looke against the Sun. The plague shall raigne mortally amongst poore men, that diuerse of them shal not be able to change a man a groate. Olde women[Pg 204] that haue taken great colde, may perhaps be trobled with the cough, and such as haue paine in their teeth, shall bee grieuouslie troubled with the tooth ach. Beside, sicke folke shall haue worse stomackes then they which be whole, and men that cannot sleepe, shall take verie little rest: with other accidentall infirmities, which I doe ouerpasse.

A declaration of the disposition and inclination of the Summer quarter.

When the Sunne hath made his course through the vernal signs, Aries, Taurus & Gemini at his passage vnto the solsticiall estiuall signe Cancer. The third parte of an English yeere called Summer, taketh his beginning this yere: as Ptolomie sayth, the twelfth of Iune, but as my skill doth coniecture, it beginneth when the wether waxeth so hot that beggers scorne barnes and lie in the field for heate, and the wormes of Saint Pancredge Church build their bowers vnder the shadow of Colman hedge. The predominant qualities of this quarter is heate and drynesse, whereby I doe gather, that through the influence of Cancer, bottle Ale shall be in great authoritie, and wheat shall doe knightes seruice vnto malte. Tapsters this quarter shall be in greater credite than Coblers, and many shall drinke more then they can yearne. And yet because Mercurie is[Pg 205] a signe that is nowe predominant, women shall be more troubled with fleas then men, and such as want meate shall goe supperlesse to bedde. Besides, this quarter great hurlie burlies are like to bee feared, and greate stratagems like to bee performed, thorough the opposition of Mars and Saturne: for Butchers are like to make great hauocke amongest flies, and beggers on Sunne shine dayes to commit great murthers vpon their rebellious vermine, and the knights of Coppersmiths hap to / doo great deedes of armes vpon Cuppes, Cannes, pots, glasses, and black iacks: not ceasing the skirmish til they are able to stand on their legges.

Further it is to bee doubted, that because Venus is in the house of Loue, that Millers, Weauers, and Taylors shall be counted as theeuishe as they are knauishe: and Maides this quarter shall make sillyebubbes for their Louers, till some of them Calue with the Cowe for companye. But Iupiter in his exaltation presageth that diuers young Gentlemen shall creepe further into the Mercers Booke in a Moneth then they can get out in a yere: and that sundry fellowes in their silkes shall be appointed to keep Duke Humfrye company in Poules, because they know not wher to get their dinner abroad: if there be great plenty of Cherries this Summer, they are like to come to a penny the pound, and Costard-mongers this Summer shall be licenst by the Wardens[Pg 206] of their hall, to weare and carry baskets of Apples on their heads to keepe them from the heat of the Sun. But Libra adust and retrograde, foretelleth that there is like to be a league between diuers bakers & the pillorye, for making their bread so light, and the Sun shall be so hotte, that it shall melt awaye the consciences of diuers couetous men, and that / by the meanes of Venus which is in the house of Scorpion, women shall bee so loue sicke, that Sumners and ciuil lawiers shall haue great fees thorough the aboundance of such sinfull clients, and diuerse spirites in white sheetes shall stand in Poules and other Churches, to make their confessions. But this by the waie learne of me, shomakers shall proue so proud that they shall refuse the name of souters, and the Tailer and the louse are like to fall at martiall variance, were it not the worshipfull company of the Botchers haue set downe this order, that he that lies in his bed while his clothes be mending, neede not haue a man to keepe his wardroppe. But amongst all, the Smithes haue put vp a supplication to the Alecunners, that he which goes dronke to bed, and as soone as hee wakes dares not carouse a hartie draught the next morning, shall drinke two daies together small Ale for his penance.

This variable season is like to bring variable accidents, for diuerse diseases which will much molest the people, namely the plurisies which shall[Pg 207] grieue many, that they shall haue farre more knauerie than they haue honestie, diuerse fluxes, and especiallie in poore mens purses, for they shall bee so laxatiue, that money shall runne out faster than / they can get it. The small pockes among children and great amongst men, infirmities in the tong, some shall doe nothing but lie with others, which I let pas.

A declaration of the inclination and disposition of the Autumnall or haruest quarter.

Haruest and the last quarter of this yeere beginneth, as I coniecture, when corne is ripe. But for the nature of this autumnall reuolution, because it beginneth in Libra, I gather there shall be more holes open this quarter then in all the yeere beside, and strange euents shall chance, for knaues shall weare smockes, and women shall haue holes in their heartes, that as fast as loue creepes in at one, it shall runne out at another. Yet Leo being a firie signe, foresheweth that diuerse men shall haue their teeth longer then their beards, and some shal be so Sun burnt with sitting in the Alehouse, that their noses shall bee able to light a candle. Others shall for want of money paune their clokes, and march mannerly in theyr doublet and their hose. And some shall this yere haue barnes and yet want corn to put in them. Rie this yeere shall bee common[Pg 208] in / England, and knaues shall be licenst to sel it by the pound, and he that wil not this quarter spend a pennie with his friende, by the counsayle of Albumazar, shall bee thrust quite out of all good companie for his labour.

It may be doubted that some straunge sicknesse and vnknowen diseases wil happen, as hollownesse of the heart, that a man shall not know a knaue from an honest man, and vncouth consumptions of the lyuer, that diuerse men of good wealth shall by their kinde hearts spend all and die banquerouts: some shal be troubled with diseases in the throate, which cannot bee helpte without Bull the hang man plaie the skilfull Chyrurgion. Amongest the rest, many that haue faire wiues shalbe troubled with greate swelling in the browes, a disease as incurable as the goute. Some shall bee troubled with the stone, and seeke to cunning women to cure them of that disease, an infirmitie easilie amended, and the doctors of Bridewell did not punish such women Phisitians by a Statute. But the greatest disease that is to bee feared, is the Cataphalusie, that is to saie, good fellowes this yeere for want of money shall oft times be contented to part companie.

And / thus (gentle reader) thou hast my prognostication, gathered by arte, and confirmed by experience, and therefore take it in good worth, for *Quod gratis grate*, and so farewell.

[Pg 209]

VII.—THOMAS DEKKER

(The Gull's Hornbook *is an almost famous work, and has, I believe, been cheaply reprinted in separate form of late years. It cannot, however, be too well known, for it is excellent in itself, and though undoubtedly paraphrased from the* Grobianus *of Dedekind, is so adjusted to English contemporary manners as to be practically original.*)

[Pg 210]

THE GVLS

Horne-booke:

Stultorum plena sunt omnia.

Al Sauio meza parola,
Basta.

By T. Deckar.

Labore et Constantia.

Imprinted at London for R. S. 1609.

[Pg 211]

To all Guls in generall, wealth and Liberty.

WHOM can I choose (my most worthie *Mecæn-asses*) to be Patrons to this labour of mine fitter thē yourselues? Your hands are euer open, your purses neuer shut. So that you stand not in the *Common Rancke* of *Dry-fisted Patrons*, (who giue nothing) for you giue all. Schollers, therefore, are as much beholden to you, as Vintners, Players, and Puncks are. Those three trades gaine by you more then Vsurers do by thirty in the hundred: You spend the wines of the one, you make suppers for the other, and change your Gold into White money with the third. Who is more liberall then you? who (but only Cittizens) are more free? Blame me not therefore, if I pick you out from the bunch of *Booke-takers*, to consecrate these fruits of my braine (which shall neuer die) onely to you. I know that most of you (O admirable *Guls*!) can neither write nor reade. A *Horne-booke* haue I inuented, because I would haue you well schooled. *Powles* is your *Walke*; but this your Guid: if it lead you right, thanke me: if astray, men will beare with your errors, because you are *Guls*. Farewell.

T. D.

[Pg 212]

To the Reader.

GENTLE *Reader, I could willingly be content that thou shouldest neither be at cost to buy this booke, nor at the labour to reade it. It is not my ambition to bee a man in Print, thus euery Tearm*; Ad prælum, tanquàm ad prælium; *Wee should come to the Presse as we come to the Field (seldome). This Tree of* Guls *was planted long since, but not taking roote, could neuer beare till now. It hath a relish of* Grobianisme, *and tastes very strongly of it in the beginning:*

the reason thereof is, that, hauing translated many Bookes of that into English Verse, and not greatly liking the Subiect, I altred the Shape, and of a Dutchman fashioned a meere Englishman. It is a Table wherein are drawne sundry Pictures: the cullors are fresh; if they be well laid on, I think my workmanship well bestowed: if ill, so much the better, because I draw the pictures onely of Guls.

T. D. /

[Pg 213]

THE GULS HORN-BOOKE:

OR

Fashions to please all sorts of Guls.

Procemium.

I sing (like the cuckooe in June) to bee laught at: if therefore I make a scuruy noise, and that my tunes sound vnmusically (the Ditty being altogether lame in respect of the bad feete, and vnhansome in regard of the worme-eaten fashion) you that haue authority vnder the broad seale of mouldy custom, to be called the *gentle Audience*, set your goodly great hands to my pardon: or else, because I scorne to be vpbraided that I professe to instruct others in an Art, whereof I my selfe am ignorant, Doe your worst: chuse whether you will let my notes haue you by the eares, or no: hisse or giue plaudities, I care not a nut-shell which of either: you can neither shake our *Comick Theater* with your stinking breath of hisses, nor raise it with the thunder-claps of your hands: vp it goes, *in dispetto del fato*. Ye motley is bought, and a[Pg 214] coat with foure elbowes (for any one that will weare it) is put to making, in defiance of the seuen wise maisters: for I haue smelt out of the musty sheetes of an olde

Almanacke, that (at one time or other) euen he that iets vpon the neatest and sprucest leather, euen he that talkes all *Adage* and *Apothegme*, euen he that will not haue a wrinckle in his new Sattein suit, though his mind be vglier then his face, and his face so illfauouredly made, that he lookes at all times as if a tooth-drawer were fumbling about his gommes with a / thousand lame *Heteroclites* more, that cozen the world with a guilt spur and a ruffled boote; will be all glad to fit themselues in *Will Sommer* his wardrob, and be driuen (like a Flemish Hoy in foule weather) to slip into our Schoole, and take out a lesson. Tush, *Cœlum petimus stultitiâ*, all that are chosen Constables for their wit go not to heauen.

A fig therefore for the new-found Colledge of *Criticks*. You Courtiers, that do nothing but sing the *gamuth-a-re* of complemental courtesie, and at the rusticall behauiour of our Countrie Muse, will screw forth worse faces then those which God and the Painter has bestowed vpon you, I defie your perfumd scorne: and vow to poyson your Muske cats, if their ciuet excrement doe but once play with my nose. You *ordinary Gulles*, that through a poore and silly ambition to be thought you inherit the[Pg 215] reuenues of extraordinary wit, will spend your shallow censure vpon the most elaborate Poeme so lauishly, that all the painted table-men about you, take you to be heires apparent to rich *Midasse*, that had more skill in *alchimy* then *Kelly* with the Phylosophers stone; (for all that he could lay his fingers on, turned into beaten gold) dry Tobacco with my leaues (you good dry brained *polipragmonists*) till your pipe offices smoake with your pittifully stinking girds shot out against me. I coniure you (as you come of the right *goose-caps*) staine not your house; but when at a new play you take vp the twelue-penny roome next the stage; (because the Lords and you may seeme to be haile fellow wel-met) there draw forth this booke, read alowd, laugh alowd, and play the *Antickes*, that all the garlike mouthd stinkards may cry out, *Away with the fool*. As for thee, Zoylus, goe hang thy selfe: and for thee *Momus*, chew nothing but hemlock, and spit nothing but the sirrup of *Aloes* vpon my papers, till thy very rotten lungs come forth for anger. I am Snake-proofe: and, though, with

Hanniball, you bring whole hogs-heads of vinegar-railings, it is impossible for you to quench or come ouer my *Alpine-resolution*: I will faile boldly and desperately alongst the shore of ye Ile of *Guls*; and in defiance of those terrible blockhouses, their loggerheads, make a true discouery of their wild (yet habitable) Country.

[Pg 216]

Sound an Allarum therefore (O thou my couragious Muse) and, like a Dutch cryer, make proclamation with thy Drum: the effect of thine O-*yes* being, That if any man, woman or child, be he Lord, be he Lowne, be he Courtier, be he Carter of ye Innes of Court, or Innes of Citty, that, hating from the bottome of his heart, all good manners and generous education, is really in loue, or rather doates on that excellent country lady, *Innocent Simplicity*, being the first, fairest, and chiefest Chamber-maide that our great *grandame Eue* entertained into seruice: Or if any person aforesaid, longing to make a voyage in the Ship of Fooles, would venture all the wit that his mother left him, to liue in the country of *Guls, cockneyes*, and *coxcombs*; to the intent that, haūting *theaters*, he may sit there, like a popiniay, onely to learne play-speeches, which afterward may furnish ye necessity of his bare knowledge, to maintaine table talke, or else, beating *tauernes*, desires to take the *Bacchanalian* degrees, and to write himselfe *in arte bibendi magister*; that at ordinaries would sit like Biasse, and in the streets walk like a braggart, that on foote longs to goe like a French Lacque, and on horsebacke rides like an English Tailor, or that from seuen yeares and vpward, till his dying day, has a monethes mind to haue ye *Guls Hornebooke* by hearte; by which in time he may be promoted to serue any Lord in *Europe*, as his crafty foole, or his [Pg 217] bawdy Jester, yea and to be so deere to his Lordship, as for the excellency of his fooling, to be admitted both to ride in Coach with him, and to lie at his very feete on a truckle-bed. Let all such (and I hope the world has not left her olde fashions, but there are ten thousand such) repaire hither. Neuer knocke (you that striue to be Ninny-hammer), but with your feete spurne open the doore, and enter into our Schoole: you shall not neede to buy bookes, no, scorne to distinguish a B from a battle doore; onely looke that your eares be long enough to reach our *Rudiments*, and you are made for euer. It is by heart that I would haue you con my lessons, and therefore be sure to haue most deuouring stomaches. Nor be you terrified with an opinion, that our *rules* be hard and indigestible, or that you shall neuer be good *Graduates* in these rare sciences of *Barbarisme*, and Idiotisme. Oh fie, vppon any man that carries that vngodly minde! Tush, tush; *Tarleton, Kemp*, nor *Singer*, nor all the litter of Fooles that now come drawling behinde them, neuer played the clownes more naturally then the arrantest Sot of you all shall if hee will but boyle my Instructions in his braine-pan.

And lest I my selfe, like some *pedantical Vicar* stammering out a most false and crackt latine oration to maister *Maior* of the towne and his brethren, should cough and hem in my deliueries; by which[Pg 218] meanes you (my Auditors) should be in danger to depart more like woodcockes then when you came to me: O thou venerable father of antient (and therefore hoary) customes, *Syluanus*, I inuoke thy assistance; thou that first taughtest Carters to weare hob-nailes, and Lobs to play Christmas gambols, and to shew the most beastly horse-trickes: O do thou, or (if thou art not at leasure) let thy Mountibancke, goat-footed *Fauni*, inspire me with the knowledge of all those silly and ridiculous fashions, which the old dunsticall world woare euen out at elbowes; draw for me the pictures of the most simple fellowes then liuing, that by their patterns I may paint the like. Awake thou noblest drunkerd *Bacchus*, thou must likewise stand to me (if at least thou canst for reeling), teach me (you soueraigne skinker) how to take the *Germanies vpsy freeze*, the Danish *Rowsa*, the Switzers stoap of *Rhenish*, the *Italians Parmizant*, the Englishmans healthes, his hoopes, cans, halfecans, Gloues, Frolicks, and flapdragons, together with the most notorious qualities of the truest tospots, as when to cast, when to quarrell, when to fight, and where to sleepe: hide not a drop of thy moist mystery from me (thou plumpest swil-bowle), but (like an honest red-nosed wine-bibber) lay open all thy secrets, and ye mystical

Hieroglyphick of *Rashers* a' th' coales, *Modicums* and *shooing-hornes,* and why they were inuented, for what occupations, and when[Pg 219] to be vsed. Thirdly (because I will haue more then two strings to my bow) *Comus*, thou Clarke of *Gluttonies* kitchen, doe thou also bid me proface, and let me not rise from table, till I am perfect in all the generall rules of *Epicures* and *Cormorants*. Fatten thou my braines, that I may feede others, and teach them both how to squat downe to their meat, and how to munch so like Loobies, that the wisest *Solon* in the world, shall not be able to take them for any other. If there be any strength in thee, thou beggerly Monarche of *Indians*, and setter-vp of rotten-lungd chimneysweepers (*Tobacco*), I beg it at thy smoaky hands: make me thine adopted heire, that, inheriting the vertues of thy whiffes, I may / distribute them amongst all nations, and make the phantastick *Englishmen* (aboue the rest) more cunning in the distinction of thy *Rowle Trinidado*, *Leafe*, and *Pudding*, then the whitest toothd Blackamoore in all *Asia*. After thy pipe, shal ten thousands be taught to daunce, if thou wilt but discouer to me the sweetnesse of thy snuffes, with the manner of spawling, slauering, spetting and driueling in all places, and before all persons. Oh what songs will I charme out, in praise of those valiantly-strong-stinking breaths, which are easily purchased at thy hands, if I can but get thee to trauell through my nose. All the foh's in the fairest Ladies mouth, that euer kist Lord, shall not fright me from thy browne pres[Pg 220]ence: for thou art humble, and from the Courts of Princes hast vouchsafed to be acquainted with penny galleries, and (like a good-fellow) to be drunke for company, with Water-men, Carmen, and Colliers; whereas before, and so still, Knights and wise Gentlemen were, & are thy companions. Last of all, thou Lady of Clownes and Carters, Schoolmistres of fooles and wiseacres, thou homely (but harmelesse) *Rusticity*, Oh breath thy dull and dunsticall spirit into our ganders quill; crowne me thy Poet, not with a garland of Bayes (Oh no! the number of those that steale *lawret* is too monstrous already) but swaddle thou my browes with those unhansome boughes, which, (like *Autums* rotten haire), hang dangling ouer thy dusty eye-lids. Helpe me (thou midwife of vnmannerlinesse) to be deliuered of this *Embryon* that lies tumbling in my braine: direct me in this hard and dangerous voyage, that being safely arriued on the desired shore, I may build up Altars to thy *Vnmatcheable Rudeness*; the excellency whereof I know will be so great, that *Grout-nowles* and *Moames* will in swarmes fly buzzing about thee. So *Herculean* a labour is this, that I vndertake, that I am enforced to ball out for all your succours, to the intent I may aptly furnish this feast of *Fooles*, vnto which I solemnely inuite all the world; for at it shall sit not only those whom *Fortune* fauours, but euen those whose wits are naturally their owne. Yet[Pg 221] because your artificiall fooles beare away the bell, all our best workmanship (at this time) shall be spent to fashion such a Creature.

CHAPTER I

The old world, & the new weighed together: the Tailors of those times, and these compared: the apparell, and dyet of our first fathers.

Good cloathes are the embrodred trappings of pride, and good cheere the very *eringo-roote* of gluttony: so that fine backes, and fat bellyes are Coach-horses to two of the seuen deadly sins: In the bootes of which Coach, *Lechery* and *Sloth* sit like the waiting-maide. In a most desperate state therefore doe Taylors, and Cookes stand, by meanes of their offices: for both those trades are Apple-squires to that couple of sinnes. The one inuents more phantasticke fashions, then Fraunce hath worne since her first stone was laid; the other more lickerish *epycurean* dishes, then were euer serud vp to *Gallonius* table. Did man (thinke you) come wrangling into the world, about no better matters, then all his lifetime to make priuy searches in Burchin lane for Whalebone doublets, or for pies of *Nightingale* tongues in *Heliogabalus* his kitchin? No, no, the first suit of apparell, that euer mortall man put on, came neither from the Mercers[Pg 222] shop nor the Merchants warehouse: *Adams* bill would haue beene taken then, sooner then a Knights bond now; yet was hee great in no bodies bookes for satten and veluets: the silkwormes had something else to do in those dayes, then to set vp loomes, and be free of the weauers: his breeches were not so much worth as K. *Stephens*, that cost but a poore noble: for *Adams* holyday hose and doublet were of no better stuffe then plaine fig-leaues, and *Eues* best gowne of the same peece: there went but a paire of sheeres betweene them. An *Antiquary* in this towne, has yet some of the powder of those leaues dryed to shew. Taylors then were none of the twelue Companies: their Hall, that now is larger then some Dorpes among the *Netherlands*, was then no bigger then a Dutch Butchers shop: they durst not strike downe their customers with large billes: *Adam* cared not an apple-paring for all their lousy hems. There was then neither the *Spanish* slop, nor the Skippers galligaskin: the *Switzers* blistred Cod-piece, nor the *Danish* sleeue sagging / down like a Welch wallet, the *Italians* close strosser, nor the French standing coller: your trebble-quadruple *Dædalian* ruffes, nor your stiffenecked *rebatoes* (that haue more arches for pride to row vnder, then can stand vnder fiue London Bridges) durst not then set themselues out in print: for the patent for starch could by no meanes be signd. Fashions then was counted a disease, and[Pg 223] horses dyed of it: But now (thankes to folly) it is held the onely rare phisicke, and the purest golden Asses liue vpon it.

As for the dyet of that *Saturnian* age, it was like their attire, homely: A sallad, and a messe of leeke porridge, was a dinner for a farre greater man then euer the *Turke* was: Potato-pies, and Custards, stood like the sinfull suburbs of Cookery, and had not a wall (so much as a handfull hie) built rownd about them. There were no daggers then, nor no Chayres. *Crookes* his ordinary, in those parsimonious dayes, had not a Capons-leg to throw at a dog. Oh golden world, the suspicious *Venecian* carued not his meate with a siluer pitch-forke, neither did the sweet-toothd Englishman shift a dozen of trenchers at one meale. Peirs ploughman layd the cloth, and Simplicity brought in the voyder. How wonderfully is the world altered? and no maruell, for it has lyein sicke almost fiue thousand yeares: So that it is no more like the old *Theater du munde*, than old *Paris* garden is like the Kings garden at *Paris*.

What an excellent workeman therefore were he that could cast the Globe of it into a new mould: And not to make it look like *Mullineux* his Globe, with a round face sleekt and washt ouer with whites of egges; but to haue it *in Plano*, as it was at first, with all the ancient circles, lines, paralels, and figures, representing indeede, all the wrinkles, crackes,[Pg 224] creuises and flawes that (like the Mole on *Hattens* cheek, being *os amoris*,) stuck vpon it at the first creation, and made it looke most louely; but now those furrowes are filled vp with Ceruse, and Vermilion; yet all will not doe, it appeares more vgly. Come, come, it would be but a bald world, but that it weares a periwig. The body of it is fowle (like a birding-peece) by being too much heated: the breath of it stinks like the mouthes of Chambermaides by feeding on so many sweat meats. And, though to purge it wil be a sorer labour then the clensing / of *Augeaes* stable, or the scowring of Mooreditch: yet, *Ille ego, qui quondam*; I am the *Pasquille madcap*, that will doot.

Draw neere therefore, all you that loue to walke vpon single and simple soules, and that wish to keepe company with none but Innocents, andΚαρηχομόωτες the sonnes of ciuill Citizens, out with your tables, and naile your eares (as it were to the pillary) to the *musique* of our instructions: nor let ye title *Gullery*, fright you frō schoole: for marke what an excellent ladder you are to clime by. How many worthy, and men of famous memory (for their learning of all offices, from the scauenger and so vpward) haue flourished in London of ye ancient familie of ye *Wiseacres*, being now no better esteemd then fooles and yonger brothers? This geare must be lookt into, lest in time (O lamentable time, when that houre-glasse is turned vp) a rich mans sonne shall no sooner peepe out of the shell of his minority but he shall straightwaies be begd for a concealement, or set vpon (as it were, by free-booters) and tane in his owne purse-nets by fencers and cony-catchers. To driue which pestilent infection from the heart, heeres a medicine more potent, and more precious, than was euer that mingle-mangle of drugs which *Mithrydates* boyld together. Feare not to tast it: a cawdle will not goe downe halfe so smoothly as this will: you neede not call the honest name of it in question, for Antiquity puts off his cap, and makes a bare oration in praise of the vertues of it: the *Receipt* hath beene subscribed vnto, by all those that haue had to doe with *Simples*, with this moth-eaten *Motto, Probatum est*: your *Diacatholicon aureum*, that with gun-powder brings threaten[ing]s to blow vp all diseases that come in his way, and smels worse then *Assafœtida* in respect of this. You therefore whose bodyes, either ouerflowing with the corrupt humours of this ages phantasticknesse, or else being burnt vp with the inflāmation of vpstart fashions, would faine be purgd: and to shew that you truly loath this polluted and mangy-fisted world, turne Timonists, not caring either for men or their maners. Doe you pledge me, spare not to take a deepe draught of our homely councel. The cup is full, and so large, that I boldly drinke a health vnto all commers. /

[Pg 226]

CHAPTER II

> How a young Gallant shall not onely keepe his clothes (which many of them can hardly doe for Brokers) but also saue the charges of taking physicke; with other rules for the morning, the praise of Sleepe, and of going naked.

You haue heard all this while nothing but the *Prologue*, and seene no more but a dumbe shew: Our *vetus Comœdia* steps out now. The fittest stage vpon which you (that study to be an Actor there) are first to present your selfe is (in my approued judgement) the softest and largest Downe-bed: from whence (if you will but take sound councell of your pillow) you shall neuer rise, till you heare it ring noone at least. Sleep, in the name of *Morpheus*, your bellyfull, or (rather) sleepe till you heare your belly grombles and waxeth empty. Care not for those coorse painted cloath rimes, made by ye Uniuersity of *Salerne*, that come ouer you, with

Sit breuis, aut nullus, tibi somnus meridianus.

Short let thy sleepe at noone be,
Or rather let it none be.

Sweete candied councell, but theres rats-bane vnder it: trust neuer a Bachiler of Art of them all, for he speakes your health faire, but to steale away the maidenhead of it: *Salerne* stands in the luxurious country of *Naples*, and who knowes not that the *Neapolitan*, will (like *Derick* the hangman) embrace you with one arme, and rip your guts with the other? theres not a haire in his mustachoo, but if he kisse you, will stabbe you through the cheekes like a ponyard: the slaue, to be auenged on his enemy, will drink off a pint of poison himselfe so that he may be sure to haue the other pledge him but halfe so much. And it may be, that vpon some secret grudge to worke the generall destruction of all mankinde, those verses were composed. *Phisisians*, I know (and none else) tooke vp the bucklers in their defence, railing bitterly vpon that venerable and princely custom of *long-lying-abed*: Yet, now I remember me, I cannot blame them; for / they which want sleepe (which is mans naturall rest) become either mere *Naturals*, or else fall into the Doctors hands, and so consequently into the Lords: whereas he that snorts profoundly scornes to let *Hippocrates* himselfe stand tooting on his Urinall, and thereby saues that charges of a groates worth of Physicke: And happy is that man that saues it; for phisick is *Non minus venefica, quam benefica*, it hath an ounce of gall in it, for euery dram of hony. Ten *Tyburnes* cannot turne men ouer ye perch so fast as one of these brewers of purgations: the very nerues of their practise being nothing but *Ars Homicidiorum*, an Art to make poore soules kicke vp their heeles. In so much,[Pg 228] that euen their sicke grunting patients stand in more danger of M. Doctor and his drugs, then of all the Cannon shots which the desperate disease it selfe can discharge against them. Send them packing therefore, to walke like *Italian Mountebankes*, beate not your braines to vnderstand their parcell-greeke, parcell-latine gibrish: let not all their sophisticall buzzing into your eares, nor their *Satyricall* canuassing of feather-beds and tossing men out of their warme blanckets, awake you till the houre that heere is prescribed.

For doe but consider what an excellent thing sleepe is: It is so inestimable a Jewel, that, if a Tyrant would giue his crowne for an houres slumber, it cannot be bought: of so beautifull a shape is it, that though a man lye with an Empresse, his heart cannot be at quiet, till he leaues her embracements to be at rest with the other: yea, so greatly indebted are we to this kinseman of death, that we owe the better tributary, halfe of our life to him: and thers good cause why we should do so: for sleepe is that golden chaine that ties health and our bodies together. Who complains of want? of woundes? of cares? of great mens oppressions, of captiuity? whilest he sleepeth? Beggers in their beds take as much pleasure as Kings: can we therefore surfet on this delicate *Ambrosia*? can we drink too much of that whereof to tast too little tumbles vs into a church-yard, and to[Pg 229] vse it but indifferently, throwes vs into Bedlam? No, no, looke vppon *Endymion*, the Moones Minion, who slept threescore and fifteene yeares, and was not a haire the worse for it. Can lying abedde till noone then (being not the threescore and fifteenth thousand part of his nap) be hurtfull?

Besides, by the opinion of all Phylosophers and Physitians, it is not good to trust the aire with our bodies / till the Sun with his flame-coloured wings, hath fand away the mistie smoake of the morning, and refind that thicke tobacco-breath which the rheumaticke night throwes abroad of purpose to put out the eye of the Element: which worke questionlesse cannot be perfectly finished, till the sunnes Car-horses stand prancing on the very top of highest noon: so that then (and not till then) is the most healthfull houre to be stirring. Do you require examples to perswade you? At what time do Lords and Ladies vse to rise, but then? your simpring Merchants wiues are the fairest lyers in the world: and is not eleuen a clocke their common houre? they finde (no doubt) vnspeakable sweetnesse in such lying, else they would not day by day put it so in practise. In a word, midday slumbers are golden; they make the body fat, the skin faire, the flesh plump, delicate and tender; they set a russet colour on the cheekes of young women, and make lusty courage to rise vp in men; they make vs thrifty, both[Pg 230] in sparing victuals (for breakefasts thereby are savd from the hell-mouth of the belly) and in preseruing apparell; for while wee warm us in our beds, our clothes are not worne.

The casements of thine eyes being then at this commendable time of the day, newly set open, choose rather to haue thy wind-pipe cut in peeces then to salute any man. Bid not good-morrow so much as to thy father, tho he be an Emperour. An idle ceremony it is, and can doe him little good; to thy selfe it may bring much harme: for if he be a wise man that knowes how to hold his peace, of necessity must he be counted a foole that cannot keep his tongue.

Amongst all the wild men that runne vp and downe in this wide forest of fooles (the world) none are more superstitious then those notable *Ebritians*, the Jewes: yet a Iewe neuer weares his cap threed-bare with putting it off: neuer bends i' th' hammes with casting away a leg: neuer cries *God saue you*, tho he sees the Diuell at your elbow. Play the Jewes therefore in this, and saue thy lips that labour, onely remember, that so soone as thy eyelids be vnglewd, thy first exercise must be (either sitting vpright on thy pillow, or rarely loling at thy bodies whole length) to yawne, to stretch,—and to gape wider then any oyster-wife: for thereby thou doest not onely send out the liuely spirits (like vaunt-currers) to fortifie and make[Pg 231] good the vttermost borders of the body; but also (as a cunning painter) thy goodly lineaments are drawne out in their fairest proportion.

This lesson being playd, turne ouer a new leafe, and (vnlesse that Freezeland Curre, cold winter, offer to bite thee) walke awhile vp and downe thy chamber, either in thy thin shirt onely, or else (which, at a bare word, is both more decent and more delectable) strip thy selfe stark naked. Are we not borne so? and shall a foolish custome make vs to breake the lawes of our Creation? our first parents, so long as they went naked, were suffered to dwell in paradice, but, after they got coates to their backes, they were turnd out of doores. Put on therefore either no apparel at all, or put it on carelessly: for looke how much more delicate libertie is then bondage, so much is the loosenesse in wearing of our attire aboue the imprisonment of being neatly and Tailor-like drest vp in it. To be ready in our clothes, is to be ready for nothing else. A man lookes as if hee be hung in chaines; or like a scarcrow: and as those excellent birds (whom *Pliny* could neuer haue the wit to catch in all his sprindges) commonly called woodcocks (whereof there is great store in England) hauing all their feathers pluckt from their backes, and being turnd out as naked as *Platoes* cocke was before all *Diogenes* his Schollers: or as the Cuckooe in Christmas, are more fit to come to any Knights board, and[Pg 232] are indeede more seruiceable then when they are lapt in their warme liueries: euen so stands the case with man. Truth (because the bald-pate her father *Time* has no haire to couer his head) goes (when she goes best) starke naked; But falshood has euer a cloake for the raine. You see likewise, that the Lyon, being the king of beasts, the horse, being the lustiest creature, the Vnicorne, whose horne is worth halfe a City; all these go with no more clothes on their backes, then what nature hath bestowed vpon them: But your babiownes, and you[r] Jackanapes (being the scum and rascality of all the hedge-creepers) they go in ierkins and mandilions: marry how? They are put into their rags onely in mockery.

Oh beware therefore both what you weare, and how you weare / it, and let this heauenly reason moue you neuer to be hansome, for, when the sunne is arising out of his bed, does not the element seeme more glorious, then (being onely in gray) then at noone, when hees in all his brauery? it were madnesse to deny it. What man would not gladly see a beautifull woman naked, or at least with nothing but a lawne, or some loose thing ouer her; and euen highly lift her vp for being so? Shall wee then abhorre that in our selues which we admire and hold to be so excellent in others?   *Absit.*

[Pg 233]

CHAPTER III

How a yong Gallant should warme himself by the fire; how attire himself: The description of a mans head: the praise of long haire.

But if (as it often happens vnlesse the yeare catch the sweating sicknesse) the morning, like charity waxing cold, thrust his frosty fingers into thy bosome, pinching thee black and blew (with her nailes made of yce) like an inuisible goblin, so that thy teeth (as if thou wert singing prick-song) stand coldly quauering in thy head, and leap vp and downe like the nimble Iackes of a paire of Virginals: be then as swift as a whirle-winde, and as boystrous in tossing all thy cloathes in a rude heape together: With which bundle filling thine armes, steppe brauely forth, crying: *Room, what a coyle keepe you about the fire?* The more are set round about it, the more is thy commendation, if thou either bluntly ridest ouer their shoulders, or tumblest aside their stooles to creepe into the chimney-corner: there toast thy body, till thy scorched skinne be speckled all ouer, being staind with more motley colours then are to be scene on the right side of the rainebow.

Neither shall it be fit for the state of thy health, to put on thy Apparell, till by sitting in that hot [Pg 234] house of the chimney, thou feelest the fat dew of thy body (like basting) run trickling down thy sides: for by that meanes thou maist lawfully boast that thou liuest by the sweat of thy browes.

As / for thy stockings and shoos, so weare them, that all men may point at thee, and make thee famous by that glorious name of a *Male-content*. Or, if thy quicksiluer can runne so farre on thy errant, as to fetch thee bootes out of S. Martens, let it be thy prudence to haue the tops of them wide as ye mouth of a wallet, and those with fringed boote-hose ouer them to hang downe to thy ankles. Doues are accounted innocent, and louing creatures: thou, in obseruing this fashion, shalt seeme to be a rough-footed doue, and be held as innocent. Besides, the strawling, which of necessity so much lether between thy legs must put thee into, will be thought not to grow from thy disease, but from that gentleman-like habit.

Hauing thus apparelled thee from top to toe, according to that simple fashion, which the best *Goose-caps* in *Europe* striue to imitate, it is now high time for me to haue a blow at thy head, which I will not cut off with sharp documents, but rather set it on faster, bestowing vpon it such excellent caruing, that, if all the wise men of *Gottam* should lay their headdes together, their Jobbernowles should not bee able to compare with thine.

To maintaine therefore that sconce of thine,[Pg 235] strongly guarded, and in good reparation, neuer suffer combe to fasten his teeth there: let thy haire grow thick and bushy like a forrest, or some wildernesse; lest those sixe-footed creatures that breede in it, and are Tenants to that crowne-land of thine, bee hunted to death by euery base barbarous *Barber*; and so that delicate, and tickling pleasure of scratching, be vtterly taken from thee: For the *Head* is a house built for *Reason* to dwell in; and thus is the tenement framed. The two Eyes are the glasse windowes, at which light disperses itself into euery roome, hauing goodly penthouses of haire to ouershadow them: As for the nose, tho some (most iniuriously and improperly) make it serue for an *Indian* chimney, yet surely it is rightly a bridge with two arches, vnder which are neat passages to conuey as well perfumes to aire and sweeten euery chamber, as to carry away all noisome filth that is swept out of vncleane corners: the cherry lippes open, like the new-painted gates of a Lord Mayor's house, to take in prouision. The tongue is a bell, hanging iust vnder the middle of the roofe; and / lest it should be rung out too deepe (as sometimes it is when women haue a peale) whereas it was cast by the first founder, but onely to tole softly, there are two euen rowes of Iuory pegs (like pales) set to keep it in. The eares are two Musique roomes, into which as well good sounds as bad, descend downe two narrow paire of[Pg 236] staires, that for all the world haue crooked windings like those that lead to the top of Powles steeple; and, because when the tunes are once gotten in, they should not too quickly slip out, all the walles of both places are plaistered with yellow wax round about them. Now, as the fairest lodging, tho it be furnisht with walles, chimnies, chambers, and all other parts of Architecture, yet, if the seeleing be wanting, it stands subiect to raine, and so consequently to ruine. So would this goodly palace, which wee haue moddeld out vnto you, be but a cold and bald habitation, were not the top of it rarely couered. Nature therfore has plaid the Tyler, and giuen it a most curious couering, or (to speake more properly) she has thatcht it all ouer, and that *Thatching* is haire. If then thou desirest to reserue that Fee-simple of wit (thy head) for thee and the lawfull heires of thy body, play neither the scuruy part of the Frenchman, that pluckes vp all by ye rootes, nor that of the spending Englishman, who, to maintaine a paltry warren of vnprofitable Conies, disimparkes the stately swift-footed wild Deere: But let thine receiue his full growth, that thou maiest safely and wisely brag 'tis thine owne *Bush-Naturall*.

And with all consider that, as those trees of cobweblawne (wouen by Spinners the fresh May-mornings) doe dresse the curled heads of the mountaines, and adorne the swelling bosomes of the [Pg 237] valleyes: Or, as those snowy fleeces, which the naked bryer steales from the innocent nibbling sheep, to make himselfe a warm winter liuery, are to either of them both an excellent ornament: So make thou account, that to haue fethers sticking heere and there on thy head, will embellish, and set thy crowne out rarely. None dare vpbraid thee, that like a begger thou hast lyen on straw, or like a trauelling Pedler vpon musty flockes: for those feathers will rise vp as witnesses to choake him that sayes so, and to proue that thy bed was of the softest downe.

When / your noblest Gallants consecrate their houres to their Mistresses and to Reuelling, they weare fethers then chiefly in their hattes, being one of the fairest ensignes of their brauery: But thou, a Reueller and a Mistris-seruer all the yeare, by wearing fethers in thy haire, whose length before the rigorous edge of any puritanicall paire of scizzers should shorten the breadth of a finger, let the three huswifely spinsters of Destiny rather curtall the thread of thy life. O no, long hair is the onely nette that women spread abroad to entrappe men in; and why should not men be as far aboue women in that commodity, as they go beyond men in others? The merry *Greekes* were called Καρηχομόωτες long-haired: loose not thou (being an honest *Troian*) that honour, sithence it will more fairely become thee. Grasse is the haire of the earth, which, so long as it is suffred to grow, it[Pg 238] becomes the wearer, and carries a most pleasing colour, but when the Sunne-burnt clowne makes his mowes at it, and (like a Barber) shaues it off to the stumps, then it withers and is good for nothing but to be trust vp and thrown amongst Jades. How vgly is a bald pate? it lookes like a face wanting a nose; or, like ground eaten bare with the arrowes of Archers, whereas a head al hid in haire giues euen to a most wicked face a sweet proportion, and lookes like a meddow newly marryed to the *Spring*: which beauty in men the Turkes enuying, they no sooner lay hold on a Christian, but the first marke they set vpon him, to make him know hees a slaue, is to shaue off all his haire close to the scull. A *Mahumetan* cruelty therefore is it, to stuffe breeches and tennis-balles with that, which, when tis once lost, all the hare-hunters in the world may sweat their hearts out, and yet hardly catch it againe.

You then, to whom chastity has giuen an heire apparant, take order that it may be apparant, and to that purpose, let it play openly with the lascivious wind, euē on the top of your shoulders. Experience cries out in euery Citty, that those self-same Criticall *Saturnists*, whose haire is shorter than their eye-brows, take a pride to haue their hoary beards hang slauering like a dozen of Foxetailes downe so low as their middle. But (alas) why should the chinnes and lippes of old men lick vp that excrement, which they[Pg 239] vyolently clip away from the heads of yong men? Is it / because those long beesomes (their beards) with sweeping the soft bosomes of their beautiful yong wiues, may tickle their tender breasts, and make some amends for their maisters' vnrecoverable dulnesse? No, no, there hangs more at the ends of those long gray haires then all the world can come to the knowledge of. Certaine I am, that when none but the golden age went currant vpon earth, it was higher treason to clip haire, then to clip money: the combe and scizers were condemned to the currying of hackneyes: he was disfranchised for euer, that did but put on a Barbers apron. Man, woman, and child woare then haire longer then a law-suit; euery head, when it stood bare or uncouered, lookt like a butter-boxes nowle, hauing his thrumbd cap on. It was free for all Nations to haue shaggy pates, as it is now onely for the Irishman. But since this polling and shauing world crept vp, locks were lockt up, and haire fell to decay. Reuiue thou therefore the old, buryed fashion, and (in scorne of periwigs and sheep-shearing) keep thou that quilted head-peece on continually. Long haire will make thee looke dreadfully to thine enemies, and manly to thy friends. It is, in peace, an ornament; in warre, a strong helmet. It blunts the edge of a sword, and deads the leaden thump of a bullet. In winter, it is a warme night-cap, in sommer, a cooling fanne of fethers.

[Pg 240]

CHAPTER IIII

How a Gallant should behaue himselfe in Powles walkes.

Being weary with sayling vp and downe alongst these shores of *Barbaria*, heere let vs cast our anchors, and nimbly leape to land in our coasts, whose fresh aire shall be so much the more pleasing to vs, if the *Ninny hammer* (whose perfection we labour to set forth) haue so much foolish wit left him as to choose the place where to sucke in: for that true humorous Gallant that desires to powre himselfe into all fashions (if his ambition be such to excell euen Complement itselfe) must as well practise to diminish his walkes, as to bee various in his sallets, curious in his Tobacco, or ingenious in the trussing vp of a new Scotch-hose: / All which vertues are excellent and able to maintaine him, especially if the old worme-eaten Farmer (his father) bee dead, and left him fiue hundred a yeare, onely to keepe an Irish hobby, an Irish horse-boy, and himselfe (like a gentleman). Hee therefore that would striue to fashion his leggs to his silke stockins, and his proud gate to his broad garters, let him whiffe downe these obseruations; for, if he once get to walke by the booke (and I see no reason but he may, as well as fight by the booke) Powles may be proud of him, *Will Clarke* shall ring forth *Encomiums* in his honour, Iohn in Powles *Church-yard*, shall fit his head for an excellent blocke, whilest all the Innes of Court reioyce to behold his most hansome calfe.

Your Mediterranean Ile, is then the onely gallery, wherein the pictures of all your true fashionate and complementall *Guls* are, and ought to be hung vp: into that gallery carry your neat body, but take heede you pick out such an hour when the maine Shoale of Ilanders are swimming vp and downe. And first obserue your doores of entrance, and your *Exit*, not much vnlike the plaiers at the Theaters, keeping your *Decorums*, euen in phantasticality. As for example: if you proue to be a *Northerne* Gentleman, I would wish you to passe through the North doore, more often (especially) then any of the other: and so, according to your countries, take note of your entrances.

Now for your venturing into the Walke, be circumspect and wary what piller you come in at, and take heede in any case (as you loue the reputation of your honour) that you auoide the *Seruing-mans* logg, and approch not within fiue fadom of that Piller; but bend your course directly in the middle line, that the whole body of the Church may appeare to be yours; where, in view of all, you may publish your suit in what manner you affect most, either with the slide of your cloake from the one shoulder, and then you must (as twere in anger) suddenly snatch at the middle of the inside (if it be taffata at the least) and[Pg 242] so by that meanes your costly lining is betrayd, or else by the pretty aduantage of Complement. But one note by the way do I especially wooe you to, the neglect of which makes many of our Gallants cheape and ordinary, that by no meanes you be seene aboue foure turnes; but in the fift make your selfe away, either in some of the / Sempsters' shops, the new Tobacco-office, or amongst the Booke-sellers, where, if you cannot reade, exercise your smoake, and inquire who has writ against this diuine weede, &c. For this withdrawing your selfe a little, will much benefite your suit, which else, by too long walking, would be stale to the whole spectators: but howsoeuer if Powles Jacks bee once vp with their elbowes, and quarrelling to strike eleuen, as soone as euer the clock has parted them, and ended the fray with his hammer, let not the Dukes gallery conteyne you any longer, but passe away apace in open view. In which departure, if by chance you either encounter, or aloofe off throw your inquisitiue eye vpon any knight or Squire, being your familiar, salute him not by his name of Sir such a one, or so, but call him *Ned*, or *Jack*, &c. This will set off your estimation with great men: and if (tho there be a dozen companies betweene you, tis the better) hee call aloud to you (for thats most gentile), to know where he shall find you at two a clock, tell him at such an Ordinary, or such, and bee sure to name those that are deerest:[Pg 243] and whither none but your Gallants resort. After dinner you may appeare againe, hauing translated yourselfe out of your English cloth cloak, into a light Turky-grogram (if you haue that happinesse of shifting) and then be seene (for a turne or two) to correct your teeth with some quill or siluer instrument, and to cleanse your gummes with a wrought handkercher: It skilles not whether you dinde or no (thats best knowne to your stomach) or in what place you dinde, though it were with cheese (of your owne mother's making) in your chamber or study.

Now if you chance to be a Gallant not much crost among Citizens, that is, a Gallant in the Mercers bookes, exalted for Sattens and veluets, if you be not so much blest to bee crost as I hold it the greatest blessing in the world, to bee great in no mans bookes) your Powles walke is your onely refuge: the Dukes Tomb is a Sanctuary, and will keepe you aliue from wormes and land-rattes, that long to be feeding on your carkas: there you may spend your legs in winter a whole after-noone: conuerse, plot, laugh, and talke any thing, iest at your Creditor, euen to his face, and in the euening, euen by lamp-light, steale out, and so cozen a whole couy of abhominable catch-pols. Neuer / be seene to mount the steppes into the quire, but vpon a high Festiuall day, to preferre the fashion of your doublet, and especially if the singing-boyes seeme to take note of you: for they are able to buzze your praises aboue their *Anthems*, if their voyces haue not lost their maiden-heads: but be sure your siluer spurres dog your heeles, and then the Boyes will swarme about you like so many white butter-flyes, when you in the open Quire shall drawe forth a perfumed embrodred purse (the glorious sight of which will entice many Countrymen from their deuotion to wondering) and quoyt siluer into the Boyes handes, that it may be heard aboue the first lesson, although it be reade in a voyce as big as one of the great Organs.

This noble and notable Act being performed, you are to vanish presently out of the Quire, and to appeare againe in the walk: But in any wise be not obserued to tread there long alone: for feare you be suspected to be a Gallant casheerd from the society of *Captens* and *Fighters*.

Sucke this humour vp especially. Put off to none, vnlesse his hatband be of a newer fashion then yours, and three degrees quainter: but for him that weares a trebled cipers about his hatte (though he were an Aldermans sonne) neuer moue to him: for hees suspected to be worse then a *Gull*, and not worth the putting off to, that cannot obserue the time of his hatband, nor know what fashioned block is most kin to his head: for, in my opinion, ye braine that cannot choose his Felt well (being the head ornament) must needes powre folly into all the[Pg 245] rest of the members, and be an absolute confirmed Foole in *Summâ Totali*.

All the diseased horses in a tedious siege cannot shew so many fashions, as are to be seene for nothing, euery day, in Duke *Humfryes walke*. If therefore you determine to enter into a new suit, warne your Tailor to attend you in Powles, who, with his hat in his hand, shall like a spy discouer the stuffe, colour, and fashion of any doublet, or hose that dare be seene there, and stepping behind a piller to fill his table-bookes with those notes, will presently send you into the world an accomplisht man: by which meanes you shall weare your clothes in print with the first edition. But / if Fortune fauour you so much as to make you no more then a meere country gentleman, or but some three degrees remoud from him (for which I should be very sorie, because your London-experience wil cost you deere before you shall haue ye wit to know what you are) then take this lesson along with you: The first time that you venture into Powles, passe through the body of the Church like a Porter, yet presume not to fetch so much as one whole turne in the middle Ile, no nor to cast an eye to *Si quis* doore (pasted and plaistered vp with Seruing-mens *supplications*) before you haue paid tribute to the top of Powles *steeple* with a single penny: And when you are mounted there, take heede how you looke downe into the yard; for the railes are as rotten as your[Pg 246] great-Grandfather; and thereupon it will not be amisse if you enquire how *Kit Woodroffe* durst vault ouer, and what reason he had for it, to put his necke in hazard of reparations. From hence you may descend, to talke about the horse that went vp, and striue, if you can, to know his keeper: take the day of the Moneth, and the number of the steppes, and suffer yourselfe to belieue verily that it was not a horse, but something else in the likenesse of one: which wonders you may publish, when you returne into the country, to the great amazement of all Farmers Daughters, that will almost swound at the report, and neuer recouer till their banes bee asked twice in the Church.

But I haue not left you yet. Before you come downe againe, I would desire you to draw your knife, and graue your name (or, for want of a name, the marke, which you clap on your sheep) in great Characters vpon the leades, by a number of your brethren (both Citizens and country Gentlemen), and so you shall be sure to haue your name lye in a coffin of lead, when yourselfe shall be wrapt in a winding-sheete: and indeed the top of Powles conteins more names then *Stowes* Chronicle. These lofty tricks being plaid, and you (thanks to your feete) being safely ariued at the staires foote againe, your next worthy worke is, to repaire to my lord *Chancellors Tomb* (and, if you can but reasonably[Pg 247] bestow some time vpon ye reading of Sir *Phillip Sydneyes* briefe Epitaph; in the compasse of an houre you may make shift to stumble it out. The great dyal is, your last monument: there bestow / some halfe of the threescore minutes, to obserue the sawciness of the Jaikes that are aboue the man in the moone there; the strangenesse of the motion will quit your labour. Besides, you may heere haue fit occasion to discouer your watch, by taking it forth, and setting the wheeles to the time of Powles, which, I assure you, goes truer by fiue notes then S. *Sepulchers* Chimes. The benefit that wil arise from hence is this, that you publish your charge in maintaining a gilded clocke; and withall the world shall know that you are a time-pleaser. By this I imagine you haue walkt your belly ful, and thereupon being weary, or (which rather I beleeue) being most Gentlemanlike hungry, it is fit that I brought you into the Duke; so (because he followes the fashion of great men, in keeping no house, and that therefore you must go seeke your dinner) suffer me to take you by the hand, and lead you into an Ordinary.

[Pg 248]

CHAPTER V

How a yong Gallant should behaue himselfe in an Ordinary.

First, hauing diligently enquired out an Ordinary of the largest reckoning, whither most of your Courtly Gallants do resort, let it be your vse to repaire thither some halfe houre after eleuen; for then you shàll find most of your fashionmongers planted in the roome waiting for meate. Ride thither vpon your galloway-nag, or your Spanish Jennet, a swift ambling pace, in your hose, and doublet (gilt rapier and poniard bestowd in their places), and your French Lackey carrying your cloake, and running before you; or rather in a coach, for that will both hide you from the basiliske-eyes of your creditors, and outrun a whole kennell of bitter-mouthed Sergeants.

Being arriued in the roome, salute not any but those of your acquaintance: walke up and downe by the rest as scornfully and as carelesly as a Gentleman-Usher: Select some friend (hauing first throwne off your cloake) to walke vp and downe the room with you, let him be suited if you can, worse by farre then your selfe, he will be a foyle to you: and this will be a meanes to publish your clothes better than Powles, a Tennis-court, or a Playhouse: discourse as lowd as you can, no matter to what purpose if you but make[Pg 249] a noise, and laugh in fashion, and haue a good sower face to promise quarrelling, you shall bee much obserued.

If you be a souldier, talke how often you haue beene in action: as the *Portingale* voyage, Cales voiage, the *Iland* voiage, besides some eight or nine imploiments in Ireland, and the low Countries: then you may discourse how honourably your *Graue* vsed you; obserue that you cal your *Graue Maurice*, your *Graue*: How often you haue drunk with Count such a one, and such a Count, on your knees to your *Graues* health: and let it bee your vertue to giue place neither to *S. Kynock*, nor to any *Dutchman* whatsoeuer in the seuenteene *prouinces*, for that Souldiers complement of drinking. And if you perceiue that the vntrauelld company about you take this downe well, ply them with more such stuffe, as how you haue interpreted betweene the French King and a great Lord of Barbary, when they haue been drinking healthes together, and that will be an excellent occasion to publish your languages, if you haue them: if not, get some fragments of French, or smal parcels of Italian, to fling about the table: but beware how you speake any Latine there: your Ordinary most commonly hath no more to do with Latine then a desperate towne of Garison hath.

If you be a Courtier, discourse of the obtaining of Suits: of your mistresses fauours, etc. Make[Pg 250] inquiry, if any gentleman at boord haue any suit, to get which he would vse ye good means of a great mans Interest with the King: and withall (if you haue not so much grace left in you as to blush) that you are (thankes to your starres) in mightie credit, though in your owne conscience you know, and are guilty to your selfe, that you dare not (but onely vpon the priuiledges of hansome clothes) presume to peepe into the presence. Demand if there be any Gentleman (whom any there is acquainted with) that is troubled with two offices; or any Vicar with two Church-liuings; which will politickly insinuate, that your inquiry after them is because you haue good means to obtaine them; yea and rather then your tongue should not be heard in the roome, but that you should sit (like / an Asse) with your finger in your mouth, and speake nothing: discourse how often this Lady hath sent her Coach for you; and how often you have sweat in the Tennis-court with that great Lord: for indeede the sweting together in *Fraunce* (I mean the society of Tennis) is a great argument of most deere affection, euen between noblemen and Pesants.

If you be a Poet, and come into the Ordinary (though it can be no great glory to be an ordinary Poet) order yourselfe thus. Obserue no man, doff not cap to that Gentleman to day at dinner, to whom, not two nights since, you were beholden for[Pg 251] a supper; but, after a turne or two in the roome, take occasion (pulling out your gloues) to haue some *Epigram*, or *Satyre*, or *Sonnet* fastned in one of them, that may (as it were vomittingly to you) offer it selfe to the Gentlemen: they will presently desire it: but, without much coniuration from them, and a pretty kind of counterfet loathnes in yourselfe, do not read it; and though it be none of your owne, sweare you made it. Mary, if you chaunce to get into your hands any witty thing of another mans, that is somewhat better, I would councell you then, if demand bee made who composed it, you may say: faith, a learned Gentleman, a very worthy friend. And this seeming to lay it on another man will be counted either modestie in you, or a signe that you are not ambitious of praise, or else that you dare not take it vpon you, for feare of the sharpnesse it carries with it. Besides, it will adde much to your fame to let your tongue walke faster then your teeth, though you be neuer so hungry, and, rather then you should sit like a dumb Coxcomb, to repeat by heart either some verses of your owne, or of any other mans, stretching euen very good lines vpon the rack of the censure: though it be against all law, honestie, or conscience, it may chaunce saue you the price of your Ordinary, and beget you other *Suppliments*. Mary, I would further intreat our Poet to be in league with the Mistresse of the Ordinary, because from her (vpon[Pg 252] condition that he will but ryme knights and yong gentlemen to her house, and maintaine the table in good fooling) he may easily make vp his mouth at her cost, *Gratis*.

Thus much for particular men. But in generall let all that are in *Ordinary*-pay, march after the sound of these directions. Before / the meate come smoaking to the board, our Gallant must draw out his Tobacco-box, the ladell for the cold snuffe into the nosthrill, the tongs and prining-Iron: All which artillery may be of gold or siluer (if he can reach to the price of it), it will bee a reasonable vseful pawne at all times, when the current of his money falles out to run low. And heere you must obserue to know in what state Tobacco is in towne, better then the Merchants, and to discourse of the Apottecaries where it is to be sold and to be able to speake of their wines, as readily as the Apottecary himselfe reading the barbarous hand of a Doctor: then let him shew his seuerall tricks in taking it, As the *Whiffe*, the *Ring*, etc. For these are complements that gaine

Gentlemen no mean respect and for which indeede they are more worthily noted, I ensure you, then for any skill that they haue in learning.

When you are set downe to dinner, you must eate as impudently as can be (for thats most Gentlemanlike) when your Knight is vpon his stewed mutton, be presently, though you be but a capten, in the [Pg 253] bosome of your goose: and when your Justice of peace is knuckle-deep in goose, you may, without disparagement to your bloud, though you haue a Lady to your mother, fall very manfully to your woodcocks.

You may rise in dinner-time to aske for a close-stoole, protesting to all the gentlemen that it costs you a hundred pounds a yeare in physicke, besides the Annual pension which your wife allowes her Doctor: and (if you please) you may (as your great French Lord doth) inuite some speciall friend of yours, from the table, to hold discourse with you as you sit in that withdrawing-chamber: from whence being returned againe to the board, you shall sharpen the wits of all the eating Gallants about you, and doe them great pleasure, to aske what Pamphlets or poems a man might think fittest to wipe his taile with (mary, this talke will be somewhat fowle if you carry not a strong perfume about you) and, in propounding this question, you may abuse the workes of any man; depraue his writings that you cannot equall, and purchase to your selfe in time the terrible name of a seuere *Criticke*; nay, and be one of the Colledge, if youle be liberall inough: and (when your turne comes) pay for their suppers.

After / dinner, euery man as his busines leades him: some to dice, some to drabs, some to playes, some to take vp friends in the Court, some to take vp money [Pg 254] in the Citty, some to lende testers in Powles, others to borrow crownes vpon the Exchange: and thus, as the people is sayd to bee a beast of many heads (yet all those heads like *Hydraes*) euer growing, as various in their hornes as wondrous in their budding and branching, so, in an Ordinary, you shall find the variety of a whole kingdome in a few Apes of the kingdome.

You must not sweare in your dicing: for that Argues a violent impatience to depart from your money, and in time will betray a mans neede. Take heede of it. No! whether you be at *Primero*, or *Hazard*, you shall sit as patiently (though you lose a whole halfe-yeares exhibition) as a disarmd Gentleman does when hees in the vnmerciful fingers of Serieants. Mary, I will allow you to sweat priuatly, and teare six or seuen score paire of cards, be the damnation of some dozen or twenty baile of dice, and forsweare play a thousand times in an houre, but not sweare. Dice your selfe into your shirt: and, if you haue a beard that your friend wil lend but an angell vpon, shaue it off, and pawne that, rather then to goe home blinde to your lodging. Further, it is to be remembred, He that is a great Gamester may be trusted for a quarters board at all times, and apparell prouided, if neede be.

At your tweluepenny Ordinary, you may giue any Iustice of peace, or yong Knight (if he sit but one[Pg 255] degree towards the Equinoctiall of the Saltseller) leaue to pay for the wine: and hee shall not refuse it, though it be a weeke before the receiuing of his quarters rent, which is a time albeit of good hope, yet of present necessity.

There is another Ordinary, to which your London Vsurer, your stale Batchilor, and your thrifty Atturney do resort: the price three pence: the roomes as full of company as a Iaile, and indeed diuided into seuerall wards, like the beds of an Hospital. The complement betweene these is not much, their words few: for the belly hath no eares: euery mans eie heere is vpon the other mans trencher, to note whether his fellow lurch him, or no: if they chaunce to discourse, it is of nothing but of *Statutes, Bonds, / Recognizances, Fines, Recoueries, Audits, Rents, Subsidies, Surties, Inclosures,* Liueries, *Inditements, Outlaries, Feoffments, Iudgments, Commissions, Bankerouts, Amercements,* and of such horrible matter, that when a Lifetenant dines with his punck in the next roome, he thinkes verily the men are coniuring. I can find nothing at this Ordinary worthy the sitting downe for: therefore the cloth shall be taken away, and those that are thought good enough to be guests heere, shall be too base to bee waiters at your Grand Ordinary; at which your Gallant tastes these commodities. He shall fare wel, enioy good company, receiue all the newes ere the post can deliuer his [Pg 256] packet, be perfect where the best bawdy-houses stand, proclaime his good clothes, know this man to drinke well, that to feed grosly, the other to swaggar roughly: he shall, if hee be minded to trauell, put out money vpon his returne, and haue hands enough to receiue it vpon any termes of repaiment: And no question, if he be poore, he shall now and then light vpon some *Gull* or other, whom he may skelder (after the gentile fashion) of mony: By this time the parings of Fruit and Cheese are in the voyder, Cards and dice lie stinking in the fire, the guests are all vp, the guilt rapiers ready to be hangd, the French Lackquey, and Irish Footeboy, shrugging at the doores, with their masters hobby-horses, to ride to the new play: thats the *Randeuous*; thither they are gallopt in post. Let vs take a paire of Oares, and now lustily after them.

CHAPTER VI

How a Gallant should behaue himself in a Play-house.

THE theater is your Poets Royal Exchange, vpon which their Muses (that are now turnd to Merchants) meeting, barter away that light commodity of words for a lighter ware then words, *Plaudites*, and the *breath* of the great *Beast*; which (like the threatnings of two Cowards) vanish all into air. *Plaiers* and[Pg 257] their *Factors*, who put away the stuffe, and make the best of it they possibly can (as indeed tis their parts so to doe), your / Gallant, your Courtier, and your Capten, had wont to be the soundest paymaisters; and I thinke are still the surest chapmen: and these, by meanes that their heades are well stockt, deale vpō this comical freight by the grosse: when your *Groundling*, and *gallery-Commoner* buyes his sport by the penny, and, like a *Hagler*, is glad to vtter it againe by retailing.

Sithence then the place is so free in entertainment, allowing a stoole as well to the Farmers sonne as to your Templer: that your Stinkard has the selfe-same libertie to be there in his Tobacco-Fumes, which your sweet Courtier hath: and that your Car-man and Tinker claime as strong a voice in their suffrage, and sit to giue iudgement on the plaies life and death, as well as the prowdest *Momus* among the tribe[s] of *Critick*: It is fit that hee, whom the most tailors bils do make roome for, when he comes, should not be basely (like a vyoll) casd vp in a corner.

Whether therefore the gatherers of the publique or priuate Play-house stand to receiue the afternoones rent, let our Gallant (hauing paid it) presently aduance himselfe vp to the Throne of the Stage. I meane not into the Lords roome (which is now but the Stages Suburbs): No, those boxes, by the[Pg 258] iniquity of custome, conspiracy of waiting-women and Gentlemen-Ushers, that there sweat together, and the couetousnes of Sharers, are contemptibly thrust into the reare, and much new Satten is there dambd, by being smothred to death in darknesse. But on the very Rushes where the Commedy is to daunce, yea, and vnder the state of *Cambises* himselfe must our fethered *Estridge*, like a piece of Ordnance, be planted, valiantly (because impudently) beating downe the mewes and hisses of the opposed rascality.

For do but cast vp a reckoning, what large cummings-in are pursd vp by sitting on the Stage. First a conspicuous *Eminence* is gotten; by which meanes, the best and most essenciall parts of a Gallant (good cloathes, a proportionable legge, white hand, the Persian lock, and a tollerable beard) are perfectly reuealed.

By sitting on the stage, you haue a signd patent to engrosse the whole commodity of Censure; may lawfully presume to be a Girder; and stand at the helme to steere the passage of *scœnes*; yet / no man shall once offer to hinder you from obtaining the title of an insolent, ouer-weening Coxcombe.

By sitting on the stage, you may (without trauelling for it) at the very next doore aske whose play it is: and, by that *Quest* of *Inquiry*, the law warrants you to auoid much mistaking: if you know not ye author, you may raile against him: and peraduenture[Pg 259] so behaue your selfe, that you may enforce the Author to know you.

By sitting on the stage, if you be a Knight, you may happily get you a Mistresse: if a mere *Fleet-street* Gentleman, a wife: but assure yourselfe, by continuall residence, you are the first and principall man in election to begin the number of *We three*.

By spreading your body on the stage, and by being a Iustice in examining of plaies, you shall put your selfe into such true *scœnical* authority, that some Poet shall not dare to present his Muse rudely vpon your eyes, without hauing first vnmaskt her, rifled her, and discouered all her bare and most mysticall parts before you at a tauerne, when you most knightly shal, for his paines, pay for both their suppers.

By sitting on the stage, you may (with small cost) purchase the deere acquaintance of the boyes: haue a good stoole for sixpence: at any time know what particular part any of the infants present: get your match lighted, examine the play-suits lace, and perhaps win wagers vpon laying tis copper, &c. And to conclude, whether you be a foole or a Justice of peace, a Cuckold, or a Capten, a Lord-Maiors sonne, or a dawcocke, a knaue, or an vnder Sheriffe; of what stamp soeuer you be, currant, or counterfet, the Stage, like time, will bring you to most perfect light and lay you open: neither are you to be hunted from thence, though the Scarcrows in the yard hoot[Pg 260] at you, hisse at you, spit at you, yea, throw durt euen in your teeth: tis most Gentlemanlike patience to endure all this, and to laugh at the silly Animals: but if the *Rabble*, with a full throat, crie, away with the foole, you were worse then a madman to tarry by it: for the Gentleman and the foole should neuer sit on the Stage together.

Mary, let this obseruation go hand in hand with the rest: or rather, like a country-seruing-man, some fiue yards before them. Present / not your selfe on the Stage (especially at a new play) vntill the quaking prologue hath (by rubbing) got culor into his cheekes, and is ready to giue the trumpets their Cue, that hees vpon point to enter: for then it is time, as though you were one of the *properties*, or that you dropt out of ye *Hangings*, to creepe from behind the Arras, with your *Tripos* or three-footed stoole in one hand, and a teston mounted betweene a forefinger and a thumbe in the other: for if you should bestow your person vpon the vulgar, when the belly of the house is but halfe full, your apparell is quite eaten vp, the fashion lost, and the proportion of your body in more danger to be deuoured then if it were serued vp in the Counter amongst the Powltry: auoid that as you would the Bastome. It shall crowne you with rich commendation to laugh alowd in the middest of the most serious and saddest scene of the terriblest Tragedy: and to let that clapper (your tongue) be tost so high,[Pg 261] that all the house may ring of it: your Lords vse it; your Knights are Apes to the Lords, and do so too: your Inne-a-court-man is Zany to the Knights, and (mary very scuruily) comes likewise limping after it: bee thou a beagle to them all, and neuer lin snuffing, till you haue scented them: for by talking and laughing (like a Plough-man in a Morris) you heap *Pelion* vpon *Ossa*, glory vpon glory: As first, all the eyes in the galleries will leaue walking after the Players, and onely follow you: the simplest dolt in the house snatches vp your name, and when he meetes you in the streetes, or that you fall into his hands in the middle of a Watch, his word shall be taken for you: heele cry *Hees such a gallant*, and you passe. Secondly, you publish your temperance to the world, in that you seeme not to resort thither to taste vaine pleasures with a hungrie appetite: but onely as a Gentleman to spend a foolish houre or two, because yoe can doe nothing else: Thirdly, you mightily disrelish the Audience, and disgrace the Author: marry, you take vp (though it be at the worst hand) a strong opinion of your owne iudgement, and inforce the Poet to take pity of your weakenesse, and, by some dedicated sonnet, to bring you into a better paradice, onely to stop your mouth.

If you can (either for loue or money) prouide your selfe a lodging by the water-side: for, aboue the conuenience it brings to / shun Shoulder-clapping,[Pg 262] and to ship away your Cockatrice betimes in the morning, it adds a kind of state vnto you, to be carried from thence to the staires of your Playhouse: hate a Sculler (remember that) worse then to be acquainted with one o' th' Scullery. No, your Oares are your onely Sea-crabs, boord them, and take heed you neuer go twice together with one paire: often shifting is a great credit to Gentlemen; and that diuiding of your fare wil make the poore watersnaks be ready to pul you in peeces to enioy your custome: No matter whether vpon landing, you haue money or no: you may swim in twentie of their boates ouer the riuer upon *Ticket*: mary, when siluer comes in, remember to pay trebble their fare, and it will make your Flounder-catchers to send more thankes after you, when you doe not draw, then when you doe; for they know, It will be their owne another daie.

Before the Play begins, fall to cardes: you may win or loose (as *Fencers* doe in a prize) and beate one another by confederacie, yet share the money when you meete at supper: notwithstanding, to gul the *Ragga-muffins* that stand aloofe gaping at you, throw the cards (hauing first torne foure or fiue of them) round about the Stage, iust vpon the third sound, as though you had lost: it skils not if the foure knaues ly on their backs, and outface the Audience; theres none such fooles as dare take exceptions at them, because, ere the play go off, [Pg 263] better knaues than they will fall into the company.

Now sir, if the writer be a fellow that hath either epigrammd you, or hath had a flirt at your mistris, or hath brought either your feather, or your red beard, or your little legs, &c. on the stage, you shall disgrace him worse then by tossing him in a blancket, or giuing him the bastinado in a Tauerne, if, in the middle of his play (bee it Pastoral or Comedy, Morall or Tragedie), you rise with a screwd and discontented face from your stoole to be gone: no matter whether the Scenes be good or no; the better they are the worse do you distast them: and, beeing on your feet, sneake not away like a coward, but salute all your gentle acquaintance, that are spred either on the rushes, or on stooles about you, and draw what troope you can from the stage after you: the *Mimicks* are beholden to you, for allowing them / elbow roome: their Poet cries, perhaps, a pox go with you, but care not for that, theres no musick without frets.

Mary, if either the company, or indisposition of the weather binde you to sit it out, my counsell is then that you turne plain Ape, take vp a rush, and tickle the earnest eares of your fellow gallants, to make other fooles fall a laughing: mewe at passionate speeches, blare at merrie, finde fault with the musicke, whew at the childrens Action, whistle at the [Pg 264] songs: and aboue all, curse the sharers, that whereas the same day you had bestowed forty shillings on an embrodered Felt and Feather (scotch-fashion) for your mistres in the Court, or your punck in the city, within two houres after, you encounter with the very same block on the stage, when the haberdasher swore to you the impression was extant but that morning.

To conclude, hoard vp the finest play-scraps you can get, vpon which your leane wit may most sauourly feede, for want of other stuffe, when the *Arcadian* and *Euphuizd* gentlewomen haue their tongues sharpened to set vpon you: that qualitie (next to your shittlecocke) is the onely furniture to a Courtier thats but a new beginner, and is but in his A B C of complement. The next places that are fild, after the Playhouses bee emptied, are (or ought to be) Tauernes: into a Tauerne then let vs next march, where the braines of one Hogshead must be beaten out to make vp another.

CHAPTER VII

How a Gallant should behaue himself in a Tauerne.

WHOSOEUER desires to bee a man of good reckoning in the Cittie, and (like your French Lord) to haue as many tables furnisht as Lackies (who, when they [Pg 265] keepe least, keepe none), whether he be a yong *Quat* of the first yeeres reuennew, or some austere and sullen-facd steward, who (in despight of a great beard, a satten suite, and a chaine of gold wrapt in cipers) proclaimes himselfe to any (but to those to whom his Lord owes money) for a ranck coxcombe, or whether he be a country gentleman, that brings his / wife vp to learne the fashion, see the Tombs at Westminster, the Lyons in the Tower, or to take physicke; or else is some yong Farmer, who many times makes his wife (in the country) beleeue he hath suits in law, because he will come vp to his letchery: be he of what stamp he will that hath money in his purse, and a good conscience to spend it, my councell is that hee take his continuall diet at a Tauerne, which (out of question) is the onely *Rende-vous* of boone company; and the Drawers the most nimble, the most bold, and most sudden proclaimers of your largest bounty.

Hauing therefore thrust your selfe into a case most in fashion (how coarse soeuer the stuffe be, tis no matter so it hold fashion), your office is (if you meane to do your iudgment right) to enquire out those Tauernes which are best customd, whose maisters are oftenest drunk (for that confirmes their taste, and that they choose wholesome wines), and such as stand furthest from ye counters; where, landing yourself and your followers, your first com [Pg 266] plement shall be to grow most inwardly acquainted with the drawers, to learne their names, as *Iack*, and *Will*, and *Tom*, to diue into their inclinations, as whether this fellow vseth to the Fencing Schoole, this to the Dauncing Schoole; whether that yong coniurer (in Hogsheads) at midnight keepes a Gelding now and then to visit his Cockatrice, or whether he loue dogs, or be addicted to any other eminent and Citizen-like quality: and protest your selfe to be extreamely in loue, and that you spend much money in a yeare, vpon any one of those exercises which you perceiue is followed by them. The vse which you shall make of this familiarity is this: If you want money fiue or six daies together, you may still pay the reckoning with this most Gentlemanlike language, *Boy, fetch me money from the barre*, and keepe yourself most prouidently from a hungry melancholy in your chamber. Besides, you shal be sure (if there be but one fawcet that can betray neate wine to the barre) to haue that arraignd before you, sooner then a better and worthier person.

The first question you are to make (after the discharging of your pocket of Tobacco and pipes, and the houshold stuffe thereto belonging) shall be for an inuentorie of the Kitchen: for it were more then most Tailor-like, and to be suspected you were in league with some Kitchen-wench, to descend your selfe, to offend your stomach with the sight of the[Pg 267] Larder, and happily to grease your Accoustrements. Hauing therefore receiued this bill, you shall (like a capten putting vp deere paies) haue many Sallads stand on your table, as it were for blankes to the other more seruiceable dishes: and according to the time of the yeare, vary your fare, as Capon is a stirring meate sometime, Oysters are a swelling meate sometimes, Trowt a tickling meate sometimes, greene Goose, and Woodcock, a delicate meate sometimes, especially in a Tauerne, where you shall sit in as great state as a Church-warden amongst his poore Parishioners, at *Pentecost* or *Christmas*.

For your drinke, let not your Physitian confine you to any one particular liquor: for as it is requisite that a Gentleman should not alwaies be plodding in one Art, but rather bee a generall Scholler (that is, to haue a licke at all sorts of learning, and away) so tis not fitting a man should trouble his head with sucking at one Grape, but that he may be able (now there is a generall peace) to drink any stranger drunke in his owne element of drinke, or more properly in his owne mist language.

Your discourse at the table must be such as that which you vtter at your Ordinary: your behauiour the same, but somewhat more carelesse: for where your expence is great, let your modesty be lesse: and, though you should be mad in a Tauerne, the largenesse of the *Items* will beare with your inciuility:[Pg 268] you may, without prick to your conscience, set the want of your wit against the superfluity and saucines of their reckonings.

If you desire not to be haunted with *Fidlers* (who by the statute haue as much libertie as *Roagues* to trauell into any place, hauing the pasport of the house about them) bring then no women along with you: but if you loue the company of all the drawers, neuer sup without your Cockatrice: for, hauing her there, you shall be sure of most officious attendance. Enquire what Gallants sup in the next roome, and if they be any of your acquaintance, do not you (after the City fashion) send them in a pottle of wine, and your name, sweetned in two pittiful papers of Suger, with some filthy Apology cramd into the mouth of / a drawer; but rather keepe a boy in fee, who vnderhand shall proclaime you in euery roome, what a gallant fellow you are, how much you spend yearely in Tauernes, what a great gamester, what custome you bring to the house, in what witty discourse you maintaine a table, what Gentlewomen or Cittizens wiues you can with a wet finger haue at any time to sup with you, and such like. By which *Encomiasticks* of his, they that know you shall admire you, and thinke themselues to bee brought into a paradice but to be meanely in your acquaintance; and if any of your endeered friends be in the house, and beate the same Iuybush that your selfe does, you[Pg 269] may ioyne companies, and bee drunke together most publikly.

But in such a deluge of drinke, take heede that no man counterfeit him selfe drunck, to free his purse from the danger of the shot: tis a usuall thing now amongst gentlemen; it had wont bee the quality of Cocknies: I would aduise you to leaue so much braines in your head as to preuent this. When the terrible Reckoning (like an inditement) bids you hold vp your hand, and that you must answere it at the barre, you must not abate one penny in any particular, no, though they reckon cheese to you, when you haue neither eaten any, nor could euer abide it, raw or toasted: but cast your eie onely vpon the *Totalis*, and no further; for to trauerse the bill would betray you to be acquainted with the rates of the market, nay more, it would make the Vintners beleeue you were *Pater familias*, and kept a house; which, I assure you, is not now in fashion.

If you fall to dice after Supper, let the drawers be as familiar with you as your Barber, and venture their siluer amongst you; no matter where they had it: you are to cherish the vnthriftinesse of such yong tame pigions, if you be a right gentleman: for when two are yoakt together by the purse strings, and draw the *Chariot* of Madam *Prodigalitie*, when one faints in the way and slips his hornes, let the other reioice and laugh at him.

[Pg 270]

At your departure forth the house, to kiss mine Hostis ouer the barre, or to accept of the courtesie of the Celler when tis offered you by the drawers, and you must know that kindnes neuer creepes vpon them, but when they see you almost cleft to the shoulders, or to bid any of the Vintners good night, is as commendable, as for a Barber after trimming to laue your face with sweete water.

To conclude, count it an honour, either to inuite or be inuited to any Rifling: for commonly, though you finde much satten there, yet you shall likewise finde many cittizens sonnes, and heirs, and yonger brothers there, who smell out such feasts more greedily then taylors hūt upon sundaies after weddings. And let any hooke draw you either to a Fencers supper, or to a Players that acts such a part for a wager; for by this meanes you shall get experience, by beeing guilty to their abhominable shauing.

CHAPTER VIII

How a Gallant is to behaue himselfe passing through the Cittie, at all houres of the night, and how to passe by any watch.

After the sound of pottle-pots is out of your eares, and that the spirit of Wine and Tobacco walkes in[Pg 271] your braine, the Tauerne door being shut vppon your backe, cast about to passe through the widest and goodliest streetes in the Cittie. And if your meanes cannot reach to the keeping of a boy, hire one of the drawers, to be as a lanthorne vnto your feete, and to light you home: and, still as you approch neere any night-walker that is vp as late as yourselfe curse and swear (like one that speaks hie dutch) in a lofty voice, because your men haue vsd you so like a rascoll in not waiting vpon you, and vow the next morning to pull their blew cases ouer their eares, though, if your chamber were well searcht, you giue onely six pence a weeke to some old woman to make your bed, and that she is all the seruing-creatures you giue wages to. If you smell a watch (and that you may easily doe, for commonly they eate onions to keep them in sleeping, which they account a medicine against cold) or, if you come within danger of their browne bils, let him that is your candlestick, and holds vp your torch from dropping (for to march after a linck is shoomaker-like), let *Ignis Fatuus*, I say, being within the reach of the Constables staffe, aske aloud, *Sir Giles*, or *Sir Abram*, will you turne this way, or downe that streete? It skils not, though there be none dubd in your Bunch; the watch will winke at you, onely for the loue they beare to armes and knighthood: mary, if the Centinell and his court of Guard stand[Pg 272] strictly vpon his martiall Law and cry stand, cōmanding you to giue the word, and to shew reason why your Ghost walkes so late, doe it in some Jest (for that will shew you haue a desperate wit, and perhaps make him and his halberdiers afraid to lay fowle hands vpon you) or, if you read a mittimus in the Constables booke, counterfeit to be a Frenchman, a Dutchman, or any other nation whose country is in peace with your owne; and you may passe the pikes: for beeing not able to vnderstand you, they cannot by the customes of the Citie take your examination, and so by consequence they haue nothing to say to you.

If the night be old, and that your lodging be some place into which no Artillery of words can make a breach, retire, and rather assault the dores of your punck, or (not to speak broken English) your sweete mistris, vpon whose white bosome you may languishingly consume the rest of darknesse that is left, in rauishing (though not restoratiue) pleasures, without expenses, onely by vertue of foure or fiue oathes (when the siege breakes vp, and at your marching away with bag and baggage) that the last night you were at dice, and lost so much in gold, so much in siluer; and seeme to vex most that two such *Elizabeth* twenty-shilling peeces, or foure such spur-ryals (sent you with a cheese and a bakt meate from your mother) rid away amongst the rest. By[Pg 273] which tragicall yet pollitick speech, you may not only haue your nighte worke done *Gratis*, but also you may take dyet there the next day, and depart with credit, onely upon the bare word of a Gentleman to make her restitution.

All the way as you passe (especially being approcht neere some of the Gates) talk of none but Lords, and such Ladies with whom you haue plaid at *Primero*, or daunced in the Presence the very same day. It is a chaunce to lock vp the lippes of an inquisitiue Bel-man: and being arriued at your lodging doore, which I would councell you to choose in some rich Cittizens house, salute at parting no man but by the name of Sir (as though you had supt with Knights) albeit you had none in your company but your *Perinado*, or your *Inghle*.

Happily it will be blowne abroad, that you and your Shoale of Gallants swum through such an Ocean of wine, that you danced so much money out at heeles, and that in wild-foule there flew away thus much: and I assure you, to haue the bill of your reckoning lost of purpose, so that it may be publisht, will make you to be held in deere estimation: onely the danger is, if you owe money, and that your reuealing gets your Creditors by the eares; for then looke to haue a peal of ordinance thundring at your chamber doore the next morning. But if either your Tailor, Mercer, Haberdasher, Silkeman, Cutter, Linen Draper,[Pg 274] or Sempster, stand like a guard of *Switzers* about your lodging, watching your vprising, or, if they misse of that, your down lying in one of the Counters, you haue no meanes to auoid the galling of their small-shot, then by sending out a light-horseman to call your Apotecary to your aide, who, encountring this desperate band of your Creditors, onely with two or three glasses in his hand, as though that day you purgd, is able to driue them all to their holes like so many Foxes: for the name of taking physicke is a sufficient *Quietus est* to any endangered Gentleman, and giues an acquittance (for the time) to them all, though the twelue Companies stand with their hoods to attend your comming forth and their Officers with them.

I could now fetch you about noone (the houre which I prescribed you before to rise at) out of your chamber, and carry you with mee into *Paules Church-yard*; where planting your selfe in a Stationers shop, many instructions are to bee giuen you, what bookes to call for, how to censure of new bookes, how to mew at the old, how to looke in your tables and inquire for such and such *Greeke*, *French*, *Italian*, or *Spanish* Authors, whose names you haue there, but whom your mother for pitty would not giue you so much wit as to vnderstand. From thence you should blow your selfe into the Tobacco-Ordinary, where you are likewise to spend your iudgment (like a[Pg 275] *Quack-saluer*) vpon that mysticall wonder, to bee able to discourse whether your *Cane* or your Pudding be sweetest, and which pipe has the best boare, and which burnes black, which breakes in the burning, &c. Or, if you itch to step into the Barbers, a whole *Dictionary* cannot afford more words to set downe notes what *Dialogues* you are to maintaine whilest you are Doctor of the Chaire there. After your shauing, I could breath you in a *Fence-schoole*, and out of that cudgell you into a *Dauncing schoole*, in both which I could weary you, by shewing you more tricks then are in fiue galleries, or fifteen prizes. And, to close vp the stomach of this feast, I could make Cockneies, whose fathers haue left them well, acknowledge themselues infinitely beholden to me, for teaching them by familiar demonstration how to spend their patrimony and to get themselues names, when their fathers are dead and rotten. But lest too many dishes should cast into a surfet, I will now take away; yet so that, if I perceiue you relish this well, the rest shall be (in time) prepared for you. *Fare-well.*

NOTES

P. 2.

The Rubie.—This is the famous and characteristic note of Euphuism—the accumulation of similes from natural history, or what was taken for natural history. It can hardly be necessary to take note of each of these; still less of the abundant classical allusions which any one acquainted with the classics will understand at once, and which could only be explained to others by loading these notes with lumps of Lemprière. Nor will any one find much difficulty in the language if he remembers that 'then' and 'than,' 'there' and 'their,' 'wayed' and 'weighed,' were written, or at least printed, in those days according to the liberal standard of the taste and fancy of the speller. In case of any difficulty, reading the word aloud will generally solve it. In a few instances, however, it may be well to gloss a little more specially.

M.—I am not sure what this abbreviates. 'Master,' for which it is the commonest sign, would do.

Oftscome = 'off-scum,' 'off-scouring.'

P. 3.

Find faulte is rather a loss: it is better than 'fault-finder.'

Closset.—This refers to the famous copy of Homer called ἡ ἐκ τοῦ νάρθηκος, which Alexander carried about with him in a sumptuous *narthex*—a portable medicine-case.

Bourde = 'jest.'

P. 5.

Parson and 'person,' interchangeably.

Cirpo, rather *scirpo*.

P. 6.

Denocated.—A mistake for either 'denotated' or 'devocated,' both possible and easily intelligible words.

Werish = 'wersh,' 'weak,' 'sickly.'

P. 7.

Predictam of course should be *praeditam*.

Presisnes, for 'preciseness,' is a good example of the quaint tricks played by phonetics.

P. 8.

Gale = gall = (in next line) *fel*.

Player.—Before his 'conversion' Gosson had himself had much to do with the theatre.

P. 11.

Plotinus.—Either Lodge or his printer has made nonsense of this. For 'Plotinus' read 'Plautus.'

P. 12.

Saphier.—Evident misprint for 'Sapphic.'

P. 16.

The quotation has been set right in some obvious matters, though not materially altered. In the second line of the English version 'with' should no doubt be 'which,' 'wh.' being the abbreviation for both.

P. 17.

Tyrtæus may perhaps be hid to some under his disguise of *Tirtheus*, which on p. 20 becomes *Tirthetus*.

P. 18.

Quinque for *quique* is very funny.

P. 19.

Stare = 'star,' 'mole.'

P. 20.

Acuate = 'sharpened,' 'spurred on.'

P. 22.

It is noteworthy that Lodge is much more eloquent and much more urgent in defence of music than of poetry, and indeed the *melomania* of the Elizabethans is well known.

P. 25.

Buggs = 'bugbears.'

Pavions = 'pavone' or 'pavine,' the well-known stately 'peacock-dance' of the time.

Dump.—Not merely as now used, 'a fit of melancholy,' but 'a melancholy tune,' and even a dance.

[Pg 280]

P. 33.

Your (Gosson) for exempting.—'Your' may be mere carelessness for 'you,' or Lodge may have at one time meant to write, 'your exempting yourself.'

P. 38.

Last line of quotation of course *contemnas* and *nam*.

P. 41.

Probably the printer gave *Silius Italicus* his *v*.

P. 44.

Pappe with an hatchet has been much discussed. The sense, which is not unlike 'giving him his gruel,' is clear enough, and any number of explanations of the form occur.

Patch. Cf. Shylock's 'The *patch* is kindly.'

P. 45.

Huffe, Ruffe, and Snuffe.—Characters in Preston's *Cambyses*. It cannot be necessary to annotate each of the plays on words of which "grating" for "greeting" is the first, and which occur throughout.

P. 46.

Ale dagger, may refer to the custom of drinking with swords on the table.

P. 47.

Scaddle is unannotated by Mr. Maskell, and does not appear in other dictionaries, even in that of Professor Skeat. But that excellent scholar, with his usual kindness, has given me a note[Pg 281] on it. It is the A.S. *scadol* from 'scathe,' and means 'mischievous,' with a secondary sense of 'thievish,' and a tertiary one of 'timid' or 'skulking.' It is here probably used in a combination of all these.

Dydoppers = 'didappers,' 'dabchicks.'

P. 51.

Bastard senior and junior are polite references to *Martin* senior and *Martin* junior, two of the pseudonyms set to the Marprelate pamphlets.

P. 52.

Elderton.—A theatrical manager.

P. 53.

Three a vies.—A 'vie' is a single stake or game at cards, or anything else. 'Three a vies' therefore equals our 'best of three.' 'Passage,' a game with dice. 'Stabbing' was a form of cogging. 'Cater-tray,' four and three. 'Cater-caps,' trencher-caps.

P. 54.

Dicker of leather.—A bundle of ten skins.

Woodsere.—Probably, as Mr. Maskell suggests, the sap that sputters from green faggots.

P. 56.

Lambacke = 'thrash.'

P. 58.

Bull.—Perhaps the hangman.

[Pg 282]

P. 64.

Aptots = 'Indeclinables.'

P. 65.

Næme, also 'eme' or 'eame' = 'uncle.'

P. 66.

Kixes or kexes.—Dry stalks of hemlock.

P. 68.

Pistle.—The common shortened form for 'epistle' much used by the Martinists.

P. 71.

Liripoope.—The *liripipium*, or long academic hood.

Chiuerell = 'doe-leather.'

P. 72.

Comedies.—Anti-Martinist plays are known to have existed, but are quite lost.

P. 76.

Muzroule or musroule.—A nose-band.

Port mouth.—I presume a kind of twitch.

Mubble fubbles = 'dumps,' 'blues.'

P. 77.

Hauncing = 'tipping.'

[Pg 283]

P. 79.

Celarent and *ferio*.—This play on the *memoria technica* of logical mood and figure is ingenious.

Ora whine meg.—Sometimes given as 'Over a whinny meg.' Name of a tune.

P. 80.

Bullen.—A vigorous pamphleteer of the preceding age.

P. 84.

Title. *Wit and Will* is the first of the 'five discourses.' Below, in the second motto, 'Vire*s*' should of course be 'vir*u*s,' being no doubt a mere misprint.

P. 86.

Gods forbod.—Dr. Grosart 'forbobod,' which appears a *vox nihili.* 'Past all gods forbod' seems to be pretty much = our 'past all praying for.'

P. 88.

Then (as constantly and not to be noticed hereafter) = 'than.'

P. 90.

Byrd. Apparently not in the sense in which 'byrd' or 'burd' is used by the ballad poets, for that is always of a girl, and Will is 'he.'

P. 100.

Buts length.—The ordinary distance between targets.

Flights shotte.—As far as the bow will carry.

[Pg 284]

P. 102.

Wood = 'mad.'

P. 109.

Will's Latin here and elsewhere is a good deal better than his modern languages.

P. 111.

Corsi[v]e = 'corrosive,' something that frets and worries.

P. 116.

Vir esset, for *virescit* apparently.

P. 134.

Labra, copies *labe*; either a mere misprint or a blunder for *labea* = *labia*, regardless of the verse. Latin is often very carelessly printed in these tracts.

P. 135.

Gray = 'badger,' from its colour.

P. 136.

Wearied.—'Weary' and 'worry' have no real connection, but the former is close in spelling and sound to 'wirian,' the O.E. form of the latter.

P. 141.

Tables = 'backgammon.'

[Pg 285]

P. 148.

Nips, etc., cant names for different classes of sharpers and thieves.

P. 149.

Ball.—Said to be a play on the proper name of Greene's mistress and her brother.

P. 150.

Place = '*locus*,' text or citation.

P. 155.

The allotment and discussion of the parts in this tirade as belonging to Marlowe and others of the earlier contemporaries of Shakespeare have employed much ink, and need no more.

P. 156.

Young Iuuenall is apparently Lodge: 'thou no lesse deseruing' Peele.

P. 166.

Barnabe Barnes, the author of *Parthenophil and Parthenophe*, was no despicable minor poet; the others were less known to fame, and a future page (175) tells most that is known about them.

P. 175.

Clarentius = 'Clarencieux.'?

P. 187.

Exitat = 'excitate,' incite.

[Pg 286]

P. 188.

Ale cunners.—'Conners or kenners,' the official inspectors of Beer.

P. 192.

A *reache* is an advantage. By 'fiue and a reache,' either card and dice sharping or pocket-picking must be meant.

P. 193.

Pullin = 'poultry.'

P. 194.

Hoffes = '*hof*,' house.

P. 195.

Here Nash takes his customary side in the Marprelate business.

P. 196.

Ram Alley, the great locality for cook-shops.

P. 198.

The *Old Swanne*, still known on the river as a pier and starting-place.

P. 199.

Heart at grasse = 'heart of grace.'

Lambeake. The simple verb 'lam,' surviving in 'lam into him,' had divers compounds—'lambaste,' 'lambeak,' (*v. ante*) and the like.

P. 202.

A return to the Martinists *dunstable*—as in 'Downright Dunstable.'

[Pg 287]

P. 205.

Duke Humfrye habitually entertained his guests in St. Paul's.

P. 208.

Cataphalusie is, I suppose, a coined word with no special meaning.

P. 212.

Full information about *Grobianisme* may be found in Chapter VII. of Mr. Herford's excellent *Literary Relations of England and Germany in the 16th Century*. Cambridge: 1886.

P. 215.

Kelly succeeded Dee as an alchemist.

P. 216.

For the *Ship of Fooles*, as Alexander Barclay Englished Sebastian Brant's *Narrenschiff*, see Mr. Herford *op. cit.*

Like Biasse = 'crookedly'?

P. 217.

Tarleton, etc.,—actors.

P. 221.

Bootes.—For the proper and original meaning of 'boot' see the opening chapter of *Old Mortality*.

P. 223.

Voyder.—The tray for sweeping off crumbs, fragments, etc., from the table.

P. 230.

Vaunt-currers = 'avant-couriers.'

P. 231.

Platoes cocke.—It was rather Diogenes's—his unfeeling jest on the 'unfeathered, two-legged animal' definition of Man.

P. 232.

Babiownes = 'baboon.'

Mandilions.—A kind of monkey.

P. 234.

Strawling = 'straddling.'

P. 242.

The *Duke*, of course Humfrye.

P. 244.

Cipers = 'cyprus,' crape.

P. 246.

Horse.—Banks's Morocco, frequent in Elizabethan mouths.

P. 273.

Perinado, guessed to = "parasite" "dinner-hunter." *Inghle* = "crony."

END

personalised classic books

UNIQUE GIFT

FOR KIDS, PARTNERS AND FRIENDS

Timeless books such as:

Kids

Alice in Wonderland • The Jungle Book • The Wonderful Wizard of Oz
Peter and Wendy • Robin Hood • The Prince and The Pauper
The Railway Children • Treasure Island • A Christmas Carol

Adults

Romeo and Juliet • Dracula

Visit **ImTheStory.com**
and order yours today!